writing with, through, and beyond the text

an ecology of language

writing with, through, and beyond the text

an ecology of language

Rebecca Luce-Kapler
Queen's University at Kingston

LEA
2004

LAWRENCE ERLBAUM ASSOCIATES, PUBLISHERS
Mahwah, New Jersey
London

Camera ready copy for this book was provided by the author.

Lawrence Erlbaum Associates, Inc., Publishers
10 Industrial Avenue
Mahwah, New Jersey 07430

Cover photo by Lynda Wilde

Cover design by Kathryn Houghtaling Lacey

Library of Congress Cataloging-in-Publication Data

Luce-Kapler, Rebecca.
Writing with, through, and beyond the text : an ecology of language / Rebecca Luce-Kapler.
p. cm.
Includes bibliographical references and index.
ISBN 0-8058-4609-3 (cloth : alk. paper)
ISBN 0-8058-4610-7 (pbk. : alk. paper)
1. English language—Rhetoric—Study and teaching. 2. English language—Composition and exercises—Study and teaching. 3. Interdisciplinary approach in education. 4. Report writing—Study and teaching. 5. Ecology—Study and teaching. 6. Nature—Study and teaching. 7. Human ecology.   I. Title.
PE1404.L83   2004
808'.042'071—dc22
2003064268
CIP

Books published by Lawrence Erlbaum Associates are printed on acid-free paper, and their bindings are chosen for strength and durability.

Printed in the United States of America
10 9 8 7 6 5 4 3 2 1

for the women with whom I have written

Contents

preface

Sooner or later ... technological civilization must accept the invitation of gravity and settle back into the land, its political and economic structures diversifying into the varied contours and rhythms of a more-than-human earth.

— David Abram

U nderstanding the potential of writing to orient us in the world, to help us think and understand, even perhaps to heal us (DeSalvo, 1999) has been the impetus behind my work as a teacher, writer and researcher and is the focus for this book. As one who works in curriculum, I follow in the manner of other curriculum theorists (Doll, 2000; Grumet, 1988; Salvio, 1999; Sumara, 2002) who question and suggest how literary processes influence learning and teaching. My work continues to raise questions for me about the presence of writing in schooling:

· How can we teach the nature of writing without committing to one process?
· Why do we often deem writing less important than reading?
· Why is the essay the privileged genre in schools?
· Why do the insights of professional writers seldom find form in literacy curricula?
· How is writing best assessed and evaluated and what are its effects?
· How do we teach the skills of writing?
· What are the benefits of writing for students?

Scholars have written many articles and books about these questions: writing processes, teaching grammar, genres of writing, and how writing should be assessed among other topics. Although many of these have useful ideas and information, much of this work seems to assume we know what writing is or that we all view it in the same way. Often the perspective is a utilitarian one: individuals need to know how to write to participate in a literate society. Whereas it is certainly true that writing is a valuable skill, I believe it is much more than that. I think that writing enriches our lives, helps us to understand who we are, and teaches us to bring closer attention to the world and even, perhaps, to change it.

I believe that, as teachers and curriculum theorists, we need to take a broader perspective toward the role of writing in our lives and understand it more fully before focusing on specific aspects; indeed, by articulating the nature of writing more clearly, some of those other questions begin to take care of themselves.

This book suggests how teachers and writers might begin to think about the phenomenon of writing, and how we can encourage *writing practices*[1] that help us interpret experience and realize new understandings. How we can write otherwise.

"Writing otherwise" is an expression that I have borrowed from Elizabeth Grosz's work. In a paper she delivered at Queen's University, Grosz explained that it was time to move beyond discussions of "writing like a woman" to think about how we could "write otherwise" (2000). She suggested that we could only change the future by changing how we articulated the past in the present. She pointed to Luce Irigaray's work, written in the future perfect tense,[2] as a way to begin to create the otherwise and for women to come into existence in the symbolic order; that is the system of human social and cultural institutions structured through language (Moi, 1985). Grosz's challenge was evocative for me since my work with women writers has made me acutely aware of the transformative possibilities of language and writing. This book begins a discussion of how such writing might occur.

To think about writing differently, I have taken up Marilyn Cooper's suggestion that writing is an ecology. A number of years ago I read her essay "The Ecology of Writing" developed from her understanding that writing engaged the individual in a variety of socially constituted and interacting systems. She noted that "an ecologist explores how writers interact to form systems: all the characteristics of any individual writer or piece of writing both determine and are determined by the characteristics of all the other writers and writings in the systems" (1986, p. 368). Cooper pointed out that some of the systems that connect writers include those of ideas, purposes, interpersonal interactions, cultural norms and textual forms. I would further add, thinking of David Abram's work in philosophy and ecology, that the locations and situations in which we write, especially ones that link us to the non-human world, also influence our work.

This conception of Cooper's has continued to stay with me as a powerful description for the processes of writing. Daily I am reminded that my writing gathers up the threads of my living and shapes them into journal entries, poems, narratives, and essays. As I begin to write this preface, for instance, I am settled in the office of a house where I have lived for only one month. Outside my window, I can see the frozen lake in the distance. Closer by, the chickadees are taking turns at the birdfeeder while the cedars near the shagbark hickory still have remnants of frost from the night. I feel the rhythms of the natural world unfolding about me in this December morning.

Somewhere in the house I can hear my daughter, Sara, who is home for the Christmas holiday. I think about her counselling work with women and the space for story that therapy creates, which brings me to think of the women writers who form the core of this book. For more than eight years, I have worked with different groups of women of all ages in research groups, writing, talking, and writing again. Threaded through these experiences are my ongoing investigations of women artists, including Emily Carr, Kate Chopin, and Margaret Bourke-White. Always, in these endeavors, I have been interested in how writing and other aesthetic practices connect us to our lived experiences and reveal the depths of those experiences.

As I consider my understanding of this work, I think about the influence of hermeneutics in my approach to writing groups.

Gadamer (1979) described how we come to our encounters with pre-judgement about how things will be (what he called "prejudice"). Through a process of dialogue and opportunities for conversation we open ourselves to partners whose understandings differ from our own and through such engagement, new interpretations emerge. The dialogue moves between our prejudices, which are revealed through conversation with someone whose perspective does not mirror our own, toward achieving some common understanding, agreement, or recognition of where disagreements lie (Crusius, 1991).

This process of interpretation is one of learning, of coming to know. Approaching one's work in such a way engages what David G. Smith called the hermeneutic imagination. Such a scholar, he noted "is not so much interested in pondering the texts and arguments of the hermeneutic tradition as engaging Life hermeneutically, which means trying to understand ever more profoundly what makes life Life, what makes living a living" (2002, n.p.). For me, expressing life through writing moves me toward understanding living.

These are just the immediate systems—nature, family, writing, other women, hermeneutics—that come easily to mind as I write. I suspect that I could make connections almost endlessly. This self-reflection, however, does illustrate the ecology of which Cooper and Abram spoke and raises my consciousness of the complexity that writing engenders and the awareness it brings me.

Writing With, Through, and Beyond the Text, drawing on many of the systems of which I am a part, considers writing as an ecology, a network of connected and nested systems within which a writer resides and works. Understanding its processes through such a lens may offer new insights into how we think about its potentials and how we might begin "writing otherwise." While one can never wholly describe the workings of such a network, by considering the small moments of writing, such as working on an individual poem, to the larger contexts of textual histories and practices, one can recognize the complexity of writing. Writing is embedded in the world and is "complex, ever unfolding, self-transcending, and relational" (Sumara et al., 2000, p. 539) and by its very nature offers the potential to write otherwise.

In forwarding this perspective of writing, I have integrated a variety of texts within this book including poetry and stories alongside academic writing and the perspectives of theorists. This style of writing is one that I have developed over time in a desire to represent my research in ways that illustrate what I am coming to know about writing. Because this book discusses how women might begin to break down some of the traditional barriers of writing to more clearly represent their experience, and indeed create new interpretive structures for that experience, I could not write this work without invoking a multiplicity of forms, voices, and structures.

The first chapter, "The Kitchen of my Imagination," begins by developing a context for the chapters that follow. I explain the research projects that inform this work and discuss the feminist theory that echoes through and shapes the book. Taking an ecological perspective means that one writing theory does not replace another; rather, traces of various theories continue to shape our understanding of writing and its processes. Therefore, a short introduction to the theories that I see most influencing this work is important.

"A Coherence of Being" begins the more detailed consideration of writing by describing the rhythm of language that recalls the rhythms of our bodies and the world. Before we begin to speak meaningful words, we develop the pattern of sound and breath. This rhythm shapes our use of language, including writing, and expresses our embodiment and connection to the natural world.

"The Language Connection" examines the nature of language as I move into thinking about semantics and how language is socially constructed. I consider the exclusion of women from the symbolic order and describe how Bahktin's explanation of the heteroglossia creates a productive opening for women. Finally, I explore a close reading of a research experience to trace some of the social, cultural and historical influences of writing.

"The Subjunctive Cottage" considers how writing, through shared cultural understandings of the role of texts, creates a subjunctive space where we can imagine new possibilities for our lives. Such a space offers the potential for exploring new rhythms, different images, and the deconstruction and reconstruction of the structures of writing. Through such processes, we may find new ways of being.

"In the Company of Writers" considers the importance of the community in writing and how the process is more collaborative than we commonly believe, even in a culture where individual production is valued. Writing groups are locations to develop a deeper understanding of our work as it is heard and recognized by others. These groups also can be sites of productive writing practices.

The final chapter, "Writing Otherwise," presents the implications of the description of writing as I have developed it, considering how we can foster writing practices that bring new learning and different understandings of our experience. Finally, I describe my vision of how understanding writing as an ecology offers the possibility of writing otherwise.

Notes

1. I use the term *writing practices* to describe the series of rituals, writing exercises, and processes in which I engage to write and which I use in my teaching of writing. Chapter six develops my conception of writing practices more fully and offers some examples.
2. The future perfect tense expresses a completed action in the future exemplified by the following: By next week I will have found my watch.

acknowledgments

This book represents many years of engagement with writing that began when I was in the third grade and my mother sent my short story to a publication that accepted work from children. When it was published, I became an author. I was fortunate to have a mother who encouraged my passion for writing and was further blessed to have several teachers who believed that writing regularly and in a variety of forms was important. In particular, I am grateful for the guidance of an English teacher, Laurene Gillard, through grades seven to ten, who created many opportunities for writing and believed in reading our work out loud. She has been a model of good teaching for me ever since.

The ecological perspective that I bring to my work was influenced by my father who has always understood how closely our fortunes are tied to the natural world and who has taught his children these lessons.

As I argue in the book, writing is a collective rather than an individual process and there have been many writers, thinkers, and colleagues who have been influential in my work and to whom I am indebted. Some are described in these chapters but many are not. Certainly the depth of such influences can never be properly recognized within the structures of a book. I am grateful for those many conversations and challenges that have improved my work.

Two colleagues and friends, in particular, have been critical in developing this thinking. Brent Davis and Dennis Sumara have included me in their interesting conversations for over ten years. Through our collaborations and other writing projects, I have come to understand more clearly my work as a teacher and writer.

Furthermore, I would like to thank Janet Miller and Donna Alvermann for their early and ongoing encouragement of this work.

I am also grateful to Leah Fowler, Wendy Atwell-Vasey and Suzanne Bratcher for their careful reading and insightful comments. Their responses enabled me to improve the quality of this work.

Naomi Silverman has been an extraordinary editor. My work has benefited greatly from her thoughtful comments and insightful suggestions. I always came away from our conversations understanding more deeply what it was I wanted to say.

I am grateful to the Social Sciences and Humanities Research Council of Canada for generous funding that has allowed me to pursue my ideas. Thank you also to the Izaak Walton Killam Memorial Scholarship and Andrew Stewart Memorial Graduate Prize committees and the Canadian Federation of University Women for the Margaret Brine Graduate Scholarship all of which supported some of this research.

Finally, many thanks to Kevin, who listened to a draft of the manuscript all the way to Chicago and who has supported me in so many other ways.

the kitchen of my imagination

The writing does not tell you everything.
Who's to say what's true and what's not?
What has been lived in my kitchen and what
in the kitchen of my imagination?[1]

My parents tell the story about how as a toddler I threw stuffed toys out of my crib to make room for the books and catalogues I preferred. Indeed, one of my earliest memories is of a bedroom dimly lit to encourage sleeping while I, sitting up in bed, page through a Sears catalogue "reading." About the same time, I became enamored with a story in an anthology that my mother brought home from the school where she taught. "Paddy's Christmas" was the tale of a small bear who refused to hibernate so that he could experience Christmas. The story just happened to contain two of my most favorite things: the holiday and the name of my babysitter, Paddy. Every day for close to a year, that was what I wanted to hear and, because I knew it so well, my poor father could not skip a page or a sentence.

These experiences and others like them began my passion for books that led to my conscious decision in elementary school to become a writer, which happened when I recognized that human beings created the stories. I had no idea how I was going to become such a person, but I knew that is what I wanted to be.

This decision shaped many important choices in my life: my emphasis on English in school; my focus on language and literacy teaching (a job that involved my passion but also, I naively thought, offered time for developing a writing career); and the research projects that I pursue. My engagement with writing and writers has influenced me in significant ways.

Writing continues to be a necessary part of my life because of its power to give shape to my knowing. I was reserved as a child and a misfit as a teenager (as many of us are), but through writing I could create a space in the world that felt like mine: my vision, my voice, my understanding of living. Through writing, I felt and continue to feel centered as I realize my thinking and develop some insight about my experience. I agree with Laurel Richardson's description of writing as a method of inquiry, a way of knowing. She explained that writing is "a method of discovery and analysis. By writing in different ways, we discover new aspects of our topic and our relationship to it" (2000, p. 923).

In writing a poem, for instance, I focus attention on specific details and the central significance of close interpretation. Creating a narrative of experience helps me re-vision its implications and connect it to other aspects of my life. Writing a book such as this brings together many threads of memory and experience and creates a meaningful coherence to my work.

Writing also reveals the contours of my subjectivity and participates in creating a sense of identity. How I understand my self is traced in part through or between the lines that I write as well as the lines and texts that write me. I am a different person when I am writing than when I am not. Clearly, according to my family, the writing me is preferable. On occasion, when my practice falls away because of other demands, someone in my family will ask, "Have you written lately?" Over the years, this statement has become a nudge that urges me back to my desk where I can re-collect myself.

When I first started teaching English, I found that I kept my writing life away from the classroom. That life included my desire for writing and a passion for immersion in story and imagery as a self-absorbed writer struggling for credibility. My school life demanded a more engaged and capable presence. Without even being aware that I was doing so, I divided writing pedagogy from my writing practice. My work with students included platitudes about finding their "writer's voice," and following "the writing process." The folly of such an existence was brought home most dramatically when

I picked up Nancie Atwell's (1987) book, *In the Middle: Writing, Reading, and Learning with Adolescents*. Over spring break, I copied the forms and planned the structures that she suggested in her book. When my students returned from the holiday, I decided, we would begin an entirely new approach to writing.

Such a dramatic shift was a disaster. I remember being in tears at the end of the first day as the system I had set in place collapsed in chaos. What I finally recognized, of course, was that only Nancie Atwell could "do" Nancie Atwell. I needed to think about how her structures could be revised to work with my teaching style, but more important was the underlying message of this experiment. I understood, finally, that I was searching for a way to bring my writing life more deeply into my work as a teacher. I recognized that the pleasures and insights that writing brought me were also important practices for my students. I did not need teachers' guides telling me how to work as a writer in a classroom. Instead, I had to pay attention to my own understandings and then consider how those might work through my teaching.

This experience was a turning point as I began to find ways to engage students in writing and excite them about English language arts. In turn, their enthusiasm encouraged me to examine writing pedagogies and processes more formally, which began with a study of junior high students in 1994. For one term, six grade seven students met with me to write and talk about their experiences of writing in school (Luce-Kapler, 1994). As we explored the writing landscape, they talked about the differences between doing such work in school and at home. Jafar summed up the feelings of many the students when he told me that his writing for the teacher was more "schooly," and that he did his better writing on his own for fun. Through the conversations, I learned that they understood the experience of creating a world through writing, but there were many things about school that impinged upon such work and made it difficult for them, not least of which was the lack of recognition that they had different preferences and processes as writers. Such diversity was not easily accommodated in more rigid curricular structures.

I knew that I wanted to continue my research in a similar vein; that is, working with groups of writers, but I was at a loss about where to go next.

Not long afterward, I was required to design a small project for an action research course. The professor suggested that we choose something directly embedded in our usual activities. I decided that since writing was my daily practice, I would form another group, but this time with peers, and I would be a participant.

I invited two women—Sidonie and Casey[2]—who also taught and wrote, and we began meeting in winter of that year. It was not long before I recognized that this structure was productive for thinking about writing, and the project grew beyond my course to become part of my dissertation work. From this association, another group evolved with adolescent girls from Sidonie's school. As my one writing group ended, the second began with Sidonie and me writing with seven young women. Here is how I described them in my research journal:

The echoes of students shouting greetings or yelling taunts, the banging lockers, the thud of books fades away. The intercom to the classroom is temporarily diverted, so the after-school announcements are faint reverberations from outside. The lights have been dimmed and nine desks are placed in a tight circle, ready for the girls to come in and settle down, their journals and bits of paper falling out of their backpacks. Alexis arrives first, bubbly and enthusiastic about returning to work with a favourite teacher and excited about writing. She is followed closely by Dale, who is younger, just in her first year of high school, and a bit shy about her writing. Ayelha arrives next, coming quietly and hesitantly into the room. She too is new to the school having moved many times in her sixteen years as a daughter of a military family. Sophia, Pegatha and Genevieve show up at the same time. Sophia is confident and outspoken about her writing, while Pegatha is very hesitant about being part of the group. Only the presence of the teacher, whom she admires greatly, relaxes her enough to stay. Genevieve is also in her first year of high school and somewhat quiet and perhaps intimidated by being in the group. Finally Norah arrives with a splash of bravado and a long speech about why she is late and why she is keen to be involved. Among the girls, as I learn afterwards, are two who are on Prozac; another is mourning the recent death of a parent. Some of the girls feel socially inept and ostracized in different ways; almost all of them feel insecure about who they are. As Sidonie, the teacher, said: "Within the insular world of an affluent, 'whitebread' suburb, the girls are trying their utmost to cope with an alarming number of issues, problems, and volatile relationships. They have difficulty negotiating the complex and confusing signals from peers, the media, their parents, counsellors, doctors, teachers and administrators."

As I moved into weekly meetings with the girls, an older woman approached me about being involved in my research study. She inquired about my work and then said, quite unexpectedly, that she would like to be involved in some way. I was surprised because I had known Carmen for a long time and had never had an indication from her that she was interested in writing.

I am still not sure what inspired her to ask, but it did open up a new vista for this research. I had worked with women in my peer group; I was working with young women; why not older women? This structure would give me a span across generations. I wanted to maintain the group structure, but knew of only one other older woman who had expressed such an interest, and she lived far away. Furthermore, Carmen was tentative and worried about her writing even though she was keen to participate. I agreed to form a group with just the two of us. With the other woman, Hazel, I maintained an email correspondence, but this was not a very satisfactory way to run a group and the data from that interaction was limited.

Each of these three writing groups had different practices. With the teachers, since we were all writers at the outset, I suggested that we bring our work-in-progress using that as a focus for our conversations about writing and teaching. This structure worked very well since we enjoyed getting specific and experienced feedback for our work. This group also contributed the most to the interpretation of the data, offering their own insights about the transcripts.

The young women's group began with Sidonie and me bringing writing practices to initiate each session. The practices tended to be about fifteen minutes in length followed by discussions about the topics that arose from this work. Later, as the girls grew more confident, they took turns bringing writing practices that they had devised. This result offered them experience in creating ongoing practices for themselves.

With the older women, I devised a series of writing prompts that they completed in reflective journal entries. With Carmen, I read her work and we met to talk about what she had written. With Hazel, as mentioned earlier, I maintained an email correspondence.

I worked with these women from 1994–1997. Since that time, I have established small groups of female graduate and undergraduate students, continuing the writing group structure that I find productive for investigating writing. This structure includes writing practices in various forms and discussion about the writing and its context. Findings from these later groups appear occasionally in this book; however, the primary focus is on the early groups where I considered the processes of women writing.

I feature two other women in this book, but they were not part of the writing groups—at least not in the way I worked with the others. These two women are artist Emily Carr and writer Kate Chopin.

When I first entered graduate studies, I was having difficulty finding structured time for what I called "my other writing"— primarily fiction and poetry. When an opportunity to engage in this writing through an independent study arose, I organized a project that included a detailed investigation of Emily Carr's artwork, her autobiographical writing, and the biographies about her. In response to these texts and pictures, I wrote journal entries and created a collection of poetry. It was the first time that I had studied another woman's life in detail, and I found the experience illuminated my understanding of my writing and my self. For instance, as I read Emily Carr's journals, I compared her aesthetic practice to my own, which brought greater awareness of interpretive structures that I was able to incorporate into my own work. Further, Carr's frustrations over public acceptance of her work highlighted for me some of the social discourses that continued to operate around notions of what women could and could not accomplish.

This project extended beyond the official end of the course to include several essays and a published collection of poetry.[3] Several years later, once the Emily Carr work had ended, I initiated a similar exploration with the work of Kate Chopin, reading her fiction and biography.

The process of deeply examining another woman's life from the perspective of her aesthetic work and the public perceptions of such work, as I develop in more detail later, has enriched my understanding of the work of women writers and brought a deeper resonance to my own writing practices.

Another important influence in my work with the women and in writing this book were my readings of feminist theory. While a number of theoretical perspectives have shaped my understanding, there are four main areas that have shaped my thinking: (1) embodied and psychological, (2) socially constructed, (3) poststructural, and (4) complex. Organizing these perspectives in such a way is somewhat artificial. Laurie Finke (1992) has posited the divisions between different fields and theories as artificially erected cultural boundaries and encouraged the circulation and exchange among them. So, although I am creating these divisions for ease in explanation, I do so suggesting that many of the ideas can shift among the categories, depending upon the context in which they are considered. What I have chosen to do is group them by what I see as their predominant character within the context of my thinking for this book.

Writing as Embodied and Psychological

The theorists who bring an embodied perspective to writing celebrate female morphology indicating, as do those who consider female psychological development, that the male has been the prototype by which everyone is measured. Historically, before society developed a two-gender model for defining difference, individuals considered male and female bodies as essentially the same with only the visibility of their genitalia providing a contrast. Over time, however, gender-specific sexual characteristics became a mark of difference that determined power structures. As that occurred, the male body became the privileged form (Oakley, 1972). The symbolic order defined women as what they were *not* rather than what they were, and described their female identities according to the roles they played for the masculine.

Luce Irigaray argued for the creation of an ethics of sexual difference that defined women in their own terms and not in relation to men. In Western culture, the conflation of "woman" with "man" has evolved to where femininity allows patriarchy to cover over the experience of women and mothers. Irigaray noted that "The law of the father needed femininity—a replica of woman—in order to take the upper hand over the mother's passion, as well as the woman's pleasure" (1991, p. 97). This psychoanalytic interpretation of the shift to patriarchy left women outside the symbolic order.

Luce Irigaray suggested that woman may find space in the symbolic order by first imagining a different metaphor where the female body is compared to elements, avoiding the dominant notion of a scopic male gaze. She spoke in terms of space, thresholds, fluids, fire and water, air and earth. Her concern was with finding representations of women in which women could find themselves or with which they could identify, a female genre.

Irigaray's most powerful and most criticized image—the "two lips"—has a wide range of interpretations from the biological evocation that metonymically recalls the female body to the metaphorical representation of the voices of women. Irigaray dismissed the recourse to anatomy or nature since women clearly have more than one pair of lips. She suggested, rather, that "it means to open up the autological and tautological circle of systems of representation and their discourse so that women may speak (of) their sex" (cited in Whitford, 1991a, p. 101). Irigaray argued that for women to have an identity, for *woman*kind to come into existence at all, depends on transgressing and subverting the symbolic. Such a change, she noted, will not leave *man*kind unchanged. She believed that woman as speaking subject, what she calls "speaking (as) woman" is something which still has to be created (Whitford, 1991b, p. 136).

Irigaray explained that women must be able to speak their identity, to speak as women within that order. She theorized that a female symbolic can emerge through the rediscovery of what she called the "maternal genealogy." This genealogy languishes in the unsymbolized mother-daughter relationship, which has a noticeable absence of representation in Western culture. Margaret Whitford, in her extensive discussion of Luce Irigaray's philosophy, suggested what recovering such a maternal genealogy might mean:

> an interpretation of the maternal genealogy ... would symbolize the relation between the girl-child and her mother in a way which allowed the mother to be both a mother and a woman, so that women were not forever competing for the unique place occupied by the mother, so that women could differentiate themselves from the mother, and so that women were not reduced to the maternal function .... I hypothesize that this alternative symbolic is not envisaged simply as a substitute for what we have now, but would be a symbolic which enabled the imaginary creative intercourse between two parents to take a symbolic form. It would be a symbolic which, by making a place for the woman, would enable cathexis of the relation *between the two parents*. It would not *replace* the paternal metaphor with a maternal one, but would allow the woman as lover, and mother as co-parent to enter the symbolic for the first time. (1991b, pp. 88–89)

Alongside Irigaray's work, we can consider other theorists who sought to counteract the psychoanalytic and psychological theories that applied the findings of male development to the experiences of women. Nancy Chodorow (1978), for example, challenged previous conceptions of female behavior when she argued that the difference between the two sexes was not because of what men could do and women could not. Rather, she saw difference as created relationally. With women the primary caretakers of children, she suggested, males had to differentiate themselves from their mothers to establish their identity while girls could relate to and identify with the mother.

Carol Gilligan (1982), building on the work of Chodorow, noted that women were missing in the work of moral development theory. In response, she studied how girls and women resolve moral dilemmas by organizing such conceptions around notions of responsibility and care. Her research was in sharp contrast to similar investigations of moral development that Kohlberg conducted with men (1984).

Mary Belenky and her collaborators (1986) further described the difference between males and females as not one of lack but one of other ways of knowing. They interviewed women in various schooling contexts and in family agencies, interested particularly in how "maternal practice might shape women's thinking about human development and the teaching relationship" (p. 13). They analyzed the transcripts from 135 interviews noting how women's self-concepts and knowing were intertwined and mapping their intellectual and ethical development. The researchers found that women repeatedly used the metaphor of voice and that "the development of a sense of voice, mind, and self were intricately intertwined" (p. 18). From this analysis, they identified five distinct ways of women's knowing: (1) *silence* as a place of not knowing, where a woman feels she has no voice or power; (2) *received knowing* where the woman trusts the knowledge of others whom she sees as more powerful and knowledgeable and from whom she can learn; (3) *subjective* knowing where the personal and private knowledge is based on intuition and feeling; (4) *procedural knowing* where the woman understands the processes and techniques for acquiring, validating, and evaluating knowledge; and (5) *constructed knowing* where the woman understands truth as contextual and knowledge as tentative rather than as absolute and where the knower constructs the known.

Emerging from the perspective of biological and psychological differences between males and females, a feminist aesthetic of writing developed. Such writing is as an erotic that comes from the self, that tends to be sensual and connected to the world and the body and that is seen to be potentially revolutionary in questioning the existing structures of literary canons and the understanding of what it means to be female. Hélène Cixous (1991), for instance, explored the connections between the sexual expression of the female body and writing; what she called *l'écriture féminine*. Cixous draws on the semiotic (those rhythmic and sensory aspects existing prior to language) associated with the female body such as its fluidity and open boundaries, shaping her writing in response and creating a woman's language. Other writers such as Adrienne Rich, Audre Lorde, and Alice Walker also work from an understanding of writing being sensual rather than abstract, "grounded in the world and in the body, creative and revolutionary" (Annas, 1987, pp. 9–10). Rich, for instance, explained:

> To think like a woman in a man's world means thinking critically, refusing to accept the givens, making connections between facts and ideas which men have left unconnected. It means remembering that every mind resides in a body; remaining accountable to the female bodies in which we live; constantly retesting given hypotheses against lived experience. (1979, pp. 244–245)

The global nature of biological and psychological categories makes it difficult to establish a specific feminist aesthetic of writing. This perspective hides many of the differences created by cultural, historical and social contexts and suggests that writing strategies are without context. Its importance lies in acknowledging that writing is embodied, that who we are shapes and is shaped by the texts we create and read and that traces of our embodied histories reside in language.

Writing as Socially Constructed

Stories such as Kate Chopin's novella, *The Awakening*, or Charlotte Perkins Gilman's story *The Yellow Wallpaper* highlighted the social constraints that structured and confined women's existence in the late nineteenth century. Into the twentieth century, Virginia Woolf wrote *A Room of One's Own* and *Three Guineas*, which critically examined the opportunities for women's intellectual work. Woolf described her struggles to learn the classical languages and literatures in order to explore the texts that were the exclusive preserve of men and allow her entrance into what was considered the educated and literary language. If one considers such cultural, historical and social influences on writing, then one can see language is not transparent or apolitical but is a site where discursive struggles occur between those that desire power through determining meaning with those that would interrupt that power for a plurality of meaning.

Since the 1970s, theorists have been describing the difficulty in representing women's experience through language that has a male-defined history. The work of Elaine Showalter (1989), for example, offered a new approach to literary criticism that would examine the ideological inscriptions of gender within texts, a process she called gynocriticism. Showalter pointed out how reading and writing by women as well as men was gendered. Later, she revised her perspective to note that the idea of a "women's culture" depended on a specific configuration or race and class and that such thinking needed to be broadened to include women of color and the urban poor (1994). In examining Showalter's work, Prins and Shreiber (1997) noted that feminist critics had moved beyond just differentiating genres of women's writing to theorizing and historicizing the differential structures of gender. Eve Sedgwick (1989) further pointed out that gender criticism could be seen as related to feminist criticism but that, in another sense, gender studies was not criticism through categories of gender but was criticism of those categories. The emergence of queer theory in the early nineties reflected this speaking and critiquing of gender, questioning constructions of masculinity, femininity, and heteronormativity.

From a social constructionist perspective, writing is a process that mediates cultural knowledge with textuality. Writers draw from ideological and discursive systems while at the same time the discourses define the choices available to them. If women construct narratives about interactions of connection while men write about separation and achievement, then they are reflecting the perceptual frameworks that have shaped them. Becoming conscious of such choices, writers may resist or subvert gender definitions and other cultural expectations.

The work of Sandra Gilbert and Susan Gubar (1979), considered one of the turning points in the study of women's writing, reveals how many genres, such as poetry and drama, erected barriers against women. Men wrote social discourse; women expressed a self through confessional pieces or disguised their work with a masculine pseudonym. Their work questioned commonsense beliefs that women prefer confessional or personal work. Rather than a quality of female nature, they explained, preference is a result of social constraints. Gilbert and Gubar highlighted how women writers nevertheless were able to create submerged or hidden meanings writing within the constraints of their time.

Susan Friedman (1994) also examined strategies that women employ to subvert genres and to claim the public space of texts. She noted that women have resisted what Virginia Woolf called "the tyranny of plot" in an accepted manner. That is, they have used the structure to write their own ideologies, such as in the rewriting of fairy tales from a feminist perspective.

Friedman also noticed that women will reconfigure narrative patterns to structure their writing in meaningful ways. For example, instead of relying on the typical rising action structure illustrated by Freytag's pyramid, they will structure a narrative recursively, returning to the same themes through different points of connection. Virginia's Woolf novel, *The Waves*, is one example of such work. Woolf wrote this book as an investigation into patterns of thinking, using the rhythms of waves rather than plot to structure the text. She told the story from the point of view of six characters interspersed with interludes that take the reader away from the focus of the individuals and to the larger world, which Woolf attempts to present as unified and coherent through the images and rhythms of the scene.

Furthermore, Friedman suggested, women whose cultures rely on a living oral tradition weave strands of oral and written narrative conventions. This observation concurs with Paula Gunn Allen who has pointed out that much of Louise Erdrich's work is such a hybridity of[*] the oral and the written. For example, *The Bingo Palace*, emerges from an oral tradition with a Western narrative gloss as does Allen's (1983) work, *The Woman Who Owned the Shadows*.[4]

Finally, Friedman explained that many women writers have reached beyond narrative to create a collaborative dialogue in their work; for instance, engaging the visual with the narrative or intertwining that narrative with lyric poetry. The collaborative dialogue also can be illustrated through the inclusion of different voices. In Rachel Blau DuPlessis's essay, "For the Etruscans," for example, she creates an essay collage with members of her workshop and with pieces from other manuscripts:

> What is going on here? 1968. Is the female aesthetic simply an (1978) enabling myth? Fish on one foot, hook on the other, angling for ourselves. Woolf: catching "something about the body."[5] Crash. MOM! WHAT! "You never buy what I like! Only what YOU like! (Fig Newtons.) (1990, p. 1)

While the social constructionist perspective of writing continues to make distinctions between female writing and male writing, it moves away from biological determinism and raises important issues about the complexity of text creation and the politics of discourse structure and use. At the same time, it encourages writers to push at boundaries and rewrite genres that more clearly represent a multitude of experiences and perspectives.

Writing as Poststructural Text

In her exploration of migrants' writing, Sneja Gunew highlights the difficulty in thinking about "women's writing":

> This controversy over whether or not women write differently simply by belonging to an unproblematic category, 'woman', still surfaces. What becomes increasingly clear is that this strategy landed us back

with biological essentialism and thus imprisoned us in a determination which precluded social change .... Women did not write differently by virtue of being born with wombs but because they had learnt to become women. (1997, p. 238)

While a social constructionist perspective acknowledges the complexity of cultural, historical and social variables that influence writing, its tendency is still to think about categories rather than how discourses create individual subjectivity, a consideration important to poststructural work. Chris Weedon (1987), in her consideration of feminist practice and poststructuralism, defined subjectivity as a woman's way of understanding herself and her relation to the world, including her conscious and unconscious thoughts and emotions, and so is constantly open to change, always shifting away from the modernist conception of a fixed and stable self at the center.[6]

While language is the site where social and political structures are defined and contested, it is also where we develop a sense of self. Using the work of Julia Kristeva, Weedon described both the symbolic and semiotic aspects of discourse, noting that rational language attempted to marginalize the semiotic in an effort to solidify meanings in the symbolic order and to create stable and unitary subjectivities. Nevertheless, language is not monolithic and can be challenged, creating an ongoing evolution. Because the subject is the site of fixing meaning, it is also the place of potential revolution.

Drawing from Foucault, Weedon explained that discourses were ways of constituting knowledge and social practices that determined forms of subjectivity and power relations. "They constitute the 'nature' of the body, unconscious and conscious mind and emotional life of the subjects they seek to govern," Weedon wrote (p. 108). For instance, one can consider how the medical community, well into the 20th century (with some vestiges still remaining in the 21st) defined notions of femininity to include images of fragility and hysteria. Such an interpretation of female health enabled the confinement of women and the controlling of their activities, profoundly illustrated in Gilman's *The Yellow Wallpaper.*

Nevertheless, Weedon pointed out, women have been able to resist such constraints and portrayals. Often this resistance is evident through their writing. Fiction is powerful in its ability to construct alternative ways of being and thinking and to bring that awareness to the discourses in which one lives. While Weedon noted that essentialist approaches assume that female authorship is the most crucial aspect of a text, poststructural theory does not guarantee that meaning is equated with authorship. Rather historical, social, and cultural contexts produce the discourses of the text. Instead of envisaging patriarchy as a fixed structure and female voices as a response, Weedon suggested that we consider patriarchal power as a web of relations with a range of feminine voices and subject positions that can support or resist such a configuration.

Bronwyn Davies is another theorist who has considered women's writing from a poststructural lens. Davies (1992) explained how poststructuralism enables one to see the self as composed of multiple and contradictory discourses that are continuous and shifting in the make up of one's subjectivity. One can maintain the illusion of a coherent self through talking about her various roles or by denying contradictions. Alternatively, one can explore the processes and discourses that constitute the self. Doing so enables one to make more conscious decisions about acting within various discourses.

Davies illustrated that such awareness brings about new storylines or metaphors that position one as a woman or revises those that have influenced her. She noted that "Much feminist writing has precisely that quality of 'bursting open' the absoluteness of experience. This is not just an angry fracturing and breaking of unwanted images and positionings—though it is also that—but the bursting forth of the bud from the death of the female winter" (p. 67). Through language we reinvent ourselves, coming to understand this process not only from reading and writing "against the grain," but also having a "detailed knowledge of the grain itself." As Wendy Hollway noted, "Consciousness-changing is not accomplished by new discourses replacing old ones. It is accomplished as a result of the contradictions in our positionings, desires and practices—and thus in our subjectivities—which result from the coexistence of the old and the new" (1984, p. 260).

Writing, from a poststructural perspective, then, is the learned social discursive practice of a gendered subject, open to negotiation and change. We find it difficult to go beyond the discursive patterns that are familiar because they are recognizable, connecting with cultural mores to seem almost natural and invisible. Nevertheless, writing is a way of coming to know and therefore can interrogate its own methods and processes. Deconstruction questions the possibility of all-encompassing systems or discourses and challenges the construction of a text, revealing the elisions and gaps. From a poststructuralist perspective, the boundaries of writing are permeable and thus texts contain elements of other discourses, genres and texts, creating an intertexual character.

Understanding writing in this way means that women can create a history by retrieving images of themselves from more dominant discourses and refashioning those images, enabling them to construct alternative interpretations. To disrupt the patriarchal structures of language and texts, some women turn to avant-garde writing with its fragmented nature and subversion of pattern as well as the strategies outlined previously by Friedman. Many of these writers are self-reflexive, deliberately drawing attention to the process of writing and the structures of the text, taking apart the inherited fabric of form and melting the boundaries between genres. Gail Scott described her inspiration for different structures coming from her dreams, which mocked the convex surface of what she thought the "real" to be. Her spare writing left spaces indicative of gaps in the culture where the feminine should be.

> the problem is in the space   the problem is in the
> space between ideology and consciousness (old systems new
> awareness   in this space was born the sentence)   the
> problem is in the space between the conscious and the un-
> conscious (once thought poetry's pure source)   out of

these two spaces in fusion has come the text but what in
rising above the others has the text left? has the text
left behind sense? has the text left behind innocence ....

(1989, p. 107)

While such writing has opened up possibilities for women to disrupt some of the patriarchal structures that confined their writing, for some women, the decentering of the self discursively is of little value if their sense of self is still uncertain. Furthermore, writers must realize that discursive practices are embedded in material power relations that also need transformation. Nevertheless, poststructural writing suggests greater possibilities for understanding the creation of subjectivity and opposing the conceptual frameworks of patriarchy.

Writing as Complex

Complexity theory underlies the ecological perspective that I am bringing to this book and understands writing as part of a web of relations that stretch beyond interpersonal interactions, cultural norms, and historical processes to non-human and subhuman systems. In a move away from Newtonian perspectives that offered mechanical metaphors for most phenomena, complexity theory supports multiple understandings and non-linear processes. Ilya Prigogine was one of the early theorists to put forward this new vision and, along with Isabelle Stengers, described the shift as a "new dialogue with nature" (1984). This dialogue reveals a world largely composed of complex systems that are spontaneous, unpredictable and volatile with new forms and patterns arising from the interaction of similar dynamic forms.

Complexity theory is the science of learning systems, systems that are open to their environment and are continually interacting with and adapting to internal and external influences and pressures. Complex systems are self-determining in that one cannot predict with complete certainty how the system will respond to influences as it draws on its past history as well as the present influences. As I type these words into the computer, I can be fairly certain how the computer will respond to my words—it will make them visible—but I can not have the same certainty when the reader encounters them. Her or his past history as well as the level of engagement with the ideas (in addition to many other factors) will shape the reader's reception. Another instance occurs at the beginning of the chapter. When my parents tried to placate a temperamental toddler by offering her books and catalogues, they would have had little idea that such an environment, fostered by story time and other interactions with texts would have led to my desire to be a writer.

While there are many examples of complex systems, one that seems most apropos for this book is that of language. As with any complex system, one can only point to some of the qualities that indicate complexity rather than exhaustively describe such a phenomenon, but briefly, language is an adapting and self-determining system in that it continually changes in response to shifting conditions and contexts and its directions cannot be predicted as some words disappear, new ones emerge, and others develop meanings opposite to their original definition. Languages that attempt to solidify usage and definition die.

Complexity theory has become a productive perspective for the field of literary theory in the past few years. Katherine Hayles (1989) was one of the first theorists to take up ideas that have become associated with complexity through her work with chaos theory. Before I proceed to describe some of Hayles's work, though, it is important to make a distinction between chaos and complexity theory. Chaos theory also studies non-linear dynamic systems but, whereas complexity theory focuses on the ability of a large number of interacting components to adapt, learn, and evolve, the former focuses on a system's sensitivity to initial conditions and the resulting effects, what Hayles called the "recursive symmetries between levels" (p. 310). Hayles provided an example of such symmetry where fluctuations at the smallest level are transmitted through the system. She described watching a river noting the large swirls of water that have smaller swirls, which have even smaller ones and so on. Most small disturbances in the water's path cancel each other out so the river flows smoothly. Occasionally, however, with the right kind of symmetry, these disturbances will be amplified to form eddies and backwaters, resulting in turbulence and complex flow patterns. In spite of such complexity, however, one can see large swirls of water that have smaller swirls within them which have smaller swirls and so on.[7]

Hayles goes on to indicate that despite claims for chaos theory overturning paradigms of totality, it still is an attempt to describe a universal structure in its tracing of influences and patterns. What interested her more is how this theory reveals a particular way of thinking in the culture and how this thinking is illustrated in literature.

Hayles illuminated this perspective by relating images and themes from Doris Lessing's *The Golden Notebook* to the ideas of chaos. The novel reflects the psychic fragmentation of Anna Wulf, who attempts to cope with her life by using different notebooks to record her experiences. This process, however, deteriorates to where Anna papers her apartment walls with newspaper clippings about horrific events, surrounding herself with chaos. From this point, Anna tries to rediscover herself as a writer through her narrative in the golden notebook. Hayles explained:

> Central to Anna's emerging reorganization is her ability to recognize recursive symmetries among and between her different notebook narratives, while still validating their local variations. After she becomes involved in a destructive relationship with a psychotic lover (Saul Green), she replays some of the scenes in another narrative with a different lover and is able to break out of the cycle because she can recognize the futility of her self-replicating assumptions. (1989, pp. 318–319)

Hayles noted that the narrative form is playing out some of the same forces that authorized chaos theory in society.

Laurie Finke (1992), inspired by the work of theorists such as Hayles who explored the intersections between science and culture, described complexity as a poetics that is cultural and indeterminate, drawing on the creative energy of chaos theory to highlight how order marginalizes, excludes and neutralizes. Finke was responding to her concern that the social constructionist view of the world as a contestable text left feminist stories with no greater claim to authority than those they had replaced. She saw in complexity a way to move from the tendency to create totalizing systems through theory. She proposed that one must engage in and challenge the competing languages of theoretical discourse. Her focus was "to articulate a dynamic description of cultural and literary activity sensitive to the complexities of gender and the semiotic practices of culture which constitute it" (p. 5). Society's many agents, discourses and institutions interact, collide and create perturbations that cannot be resolved into coherent narratives. This recognition of contingency, however, does not need to be disabling, Finke noted. Rather, it "can create the impetus to challenge hegemonic, totalizing constructions of self and society" (p. 10).

In considering writing from the perspectives of complexity theory, it is important to examine competing discourses and engage in debates without resorting to essentialism, binary division, or uncritical assimilation. Writing is not a totalizing system that renders differences and contradictions invisible but rather is part of ever-emerging cultural production that feeds back into society and contributes to its shaping.

Because complexity theory moves us away from searching for a "theory of everything," the dialogues with other literary theories enter into the discussion and become part of the dynamic process of understanding the character of writing. Noticing the influences of such theories on writing brings one to see the complexity of such a process, to identify discourses that create and modify societal practices and to recognize some of the interacting systems that shape our writing and subjectivity even as our engagement with its processes influences writing itself.

Throughout the book, while complexity is the perspective I am using to consider writing, elements of these other conceptions—

embodied and psychological, socially constructed, and poststructural—are present through the responses of the writers and my discussions of the work. An ecological approach acknowledges that these views are part of the history that has shaped writing practices and that continue to influence it, and therefore cannot be separated from the discussion. While engaging in such a dialogue, I invite the reader to consider Katherine Hayles' suggestion that theories reveal the assumptions and practices at work in culture and to consider how exploring the systems of writing can bring us insight beyond understanding its processes.

Notes

1. From R. Luce-Kapler, 1997a.
2. All the women from the studies have pseudonyms; the girls chose their own.
3. See, for example, *The gardens where she dreams* (2003), Ottawa, ON: Borealis Press and The breath of interpreting moments (2002), in E. Mirochnik & D. Sherman (Eds.), *Passion and pedagogy*. New York: Peter Lang (pp. 285–300).
4. Paula Gunn Allen presented these ideas at a public lecture, University of Alberta, September, 1996.
5. DuPlessis is here citing Virginia Woolf in Professions for Women in *The Death of the Moth and Other Essays*, 1942, reprint ed., New York: Harcourt Brace Jovanovich, 1974, p. 240.
6. Weedon's definition is one I share for my understanding of subjectivity in this book.
7. For a more detailed discussion about the differences between chaos theory and complexity see Paul Cillier (1998) *Complexity and Postmodernism* and Brent Davis (2004) *Inventions of Teaching*.

a coherence of being

What makes a lyric ring true is not catchy rhythms or mellifluous sounds, but the intuition of a coherence of being. That makes a single, singing self possible again—or at least glimpsable—in empathetic response. And lyrical rhythms and phrasings spring from that intuition; they are its sacramental embodiment.

— Dennis Lee

I grew up in an extended family where stories were a staple of our gatherings. The threads of narrative that found form and sustenance around our table shaped my early sense of who our family had been, who it was now and who it was likely to be. From these stories, an entire mythology developed about my grandfather and his friend in their travels across the United States in a Model T in the early 1900s and about their trials at farming in the Canadian West later in the 1920s. My father continued these stories and added others about the rural Alberta community of his youth. He also wove in details of relatives whom I had never seen and who lived in faraway places like Washington, Michigan and Florida.

These stories were an important background to my childhood not only because they were told with some regularity, but also because they had their own particular space and time of telling. They depended on the gathering of family over food and the rhythm of the teller's voice shifting from its everyday cadence. The storytellers emphasized some words and whispered others, their pacing calling our attention, the pauses artful and suspenseful; and they were always conscious of audience—a particular aside or a quiet wink when one of the great uncles was present or some judicious editing for the children. No matter what small adjustments, though, the stories were familiar, their structure and pattern remaining consistent. It was in the telling that the novelty would arise, the surprise would come and a new twist become part of the story's history.

With such an early immersion in storytelling, I expected to tell stories that drew from these patterns and was astonished when mine were not successful. Where the build-up to the exciting finish should come, my version fell flat. When I worked to develop familiar rhythms, my pauses felt awkward and my pacing artificial. I struggled with my deep desire to tell stories and my seeming lack of ability to do so.

What I had not recognized, though, was that the men primarily had told those stories about themselves, and that heroic structure of telling did not work for me. In my search for other ways to tell my stories, I needed rhythms that were subtler. Instead of those that depended on the collective attention to find their timbre, I was drawn to narratives that were unassuming and less intense, ones like those I had heard most often from my mother and her family.

My mother's stories came from a people used to quiet and prayerful communion rather than energetic gatherings and conversations. These were the ones that appealed to me because they seemed so tenuous, so risky. Each one built on its relationship with the next, carefully and deliberately told by women describing the struggle of a family to maintain those relationships and their faith as they immigrated to a new country. The rhythms of those stories recounted the music of the Moravian hymns, the echo of voices from Volhynia to Alberta, the steady thump of fists kneading dough and the scrape of knuckles washing clothing.

One of the early stories was about the circumstances of my birth shared with me when my mother handed me a sheaf of typewritten pages, inviting me to read what she had written.

In the aftermath of my coming my mother had developed a life-threatening blood clot. The staff in the rural hospital where I was born struggled to deal with unfamiliar oxygen technology and new drugs to slow down my mother's bodily activity so that the blood clot would not jar loose and stop the heart. My mother described reaching a crisis point and feeling suspended in emptiness, trying to grasp something tangible but being utterly frustrated until she passed into darkness. She felt herself transported by some invisible means to an unfamiliar place to join a waiting throng of people where she felt peace and contentment, in harmony with all her fellow beings. Then the vision of what she thought was heaven ended abruptly, and she became aware of her hospital surroundings. She wrote: "I felt as if I had been snatched back from the very threshold of eternity; my earthly life yet incomplete."

When my mother gave me this story to read, I was astounded. I had been part of her most tenuous moments of life and yet had had no knowledge that I was involved in such a drama. My aunt, who had been my mother's nurse, added to the story, explaining that she had tried to help by holding me to my mother's breast so that I could eat and with the easing of my mother's fullness, give her some small comfort, calming her restlessness.

What must it have been like, I have often wondered since, to have had those warm arms of my aunt, holding me up to the still and cooling breast of my mother? Was I aware of the two heartbeats of women who loved me: the slowing of one toward death, the other speeding in anxiety at its nearness? What kind of syncopation did my body experience as I absorbed those early stirrings of my life?

Susanne Langer (1953/1967) wrote that it is the rhythms of life, organic, emotional and mental that compose a dynamic pattern of feeling. Hearing the story of my aunt holding me to my mother's breast explained such a strong thread in my life—my swinging between stability and risk, liking to be out on a limb while still being held by strong hands. If my mother had held me to her breast, would I have recognized the body rhythms of my gestation, felt a greater sense of coherence? I can never know for sure, but I do believe all such experiences engage our bodies in a rhythmic relation, reminding us that we are part of the complexity of life.

In this chapter, I explore rhythm and its relationship to writing; that is how we first feel the embodied character of writing through the rhythm enacted by the repetition of sound, syllable and image. This awareness developed in part through my work exploring Emily Carr but also through my writing group experiences that illustrated how the rhythm of writing helps us interpret our lived experience and our sense of subjectivity.

The Character of Rhythm

Rhythm pervades our lives; it is essential not only for our continued existence but also for our pleasures in life. We sway and stamp our feet to the beat of music; we enjoy the falling away of mechanical time when we leave on vacation; the systems of our bodies are healthy when they work in rhythm; we recognize the cadence of a lover's voice; we appreciate the pattern of waves across a lake. The philosopher Alfred North Whitehead (1925) wrote about the essence of rhythm being a fusion of sameness and novelty. The sameness creates a unity of pattern while the novelty arises from the detail joined in a balance. If there is too much pattern, rhythm disappears, Whitehead explained, such as in a crystal. Or, if there is too much detail without pattern, such as in fog, rhythm melts away. With rhythm we live in a dynamic tension between expectation and enactment, learning to anticipate and plan within the momentum of surprise and change. We enjoy the predictability and pattern to our days even while we long for surprise or decide how to respond to unforeseen challenges.

One of our most constant reminders of rhythm is time, not the mechanical ticking of a clock or some other regular measure, but rather the lived experience of our days. Virginia Woolf suggested "that the real significance of time lies within the realm of the subtle, human interactions and enfolded, multi-layered moments of human contact" (cited in Briggs & Peat, 1999, p. 131). Such a notion of time acknowledges that while there is a sense of us living in time in a coherent way, the differences come in the day-to-day relations—the novelty of the detail.

When we pay attention to the qualitative experience of time, the dimensions open up from a strictly linear perspective to one that becomes more spatial, moments nested within moments. Christopher Bamford described such a sense of time in an essay about the death of his wife: "Time became a set of Chinese boxes, in which each moment, each movement, contained others within others, like a fugue within a fugue, so that I thought if I could but unpack one it would contain all" (2000, p. 3). The present moment contains infinite moments past, both remembered and forgotten, making possible the multiple interpretations of memory and history.

Language reflects, responds to, and shapes the rhythm of our lives. It is in the rhythm of language, Susanne Langer wrote, where there is a "mysterious trait that probably bespeaks biological unities of thought and feeling which are entirely unexplored yet" (p. 258). In oral language, one can hear the cadences of sentences, the stresses of syllables, the breathing patterns of the speaker. In written language, particularly in carefully crafted work such as poetry, rhythm arises from the diction and syllabication of words, the syntax, the relationship between text and space on the page, and the images the words evoke.

Dennis Lee (1998) illustrated such workings in his essay "Body Music." Beginning with metrical poetry, such as that using iambic pentameter, he described the syncopation where the spoken stresses of words are a counterpoint to the regular metrical beat, creating a relationship between what is fixed and what is variable. Such a rhythm develops a sense of coherence while continuing to interest the reader in the tension or novelty between the expected pattern and the stress of the words.

A simple demonstration can provide an example of how such tension is so important in poetry. Below is the opening line from one of my poems that exemplifies iambic pentameter, a pattern of two syllable stresses, the second of which is accented. If one reads the line aloud scanning it to discover the iambic emphases, and then reads it aloud as it would normally be spoken, the differences become clear.

An edge of panic runs the line of stone.

With the first reading, the over emphasis on the stressed syllables makes the line seem awkward and unpleasant to hear while on the second, the rhythm slips into the background giving a sense of coherence to a more evocative line. In reading without focusing solely on the rhythm, the balance between sameness and novelty draws our interest in the poem.

As with metrical verse, free verse depends on this kind of relation. In such poetry, however, there is not the play between the fixed and variable, but rather, as Lee pointed out, interplay among the variable systems of order. That is, patterns of speech work in relation to line breaks and layout—the margins, the internal line space and white space. From such interactions, a sense of overall pattern co-emerges with the details creating the pleasure of surprise in an interesting rhythm.

The rhythms of my mother's narratives, her careful telling of moments, was what I tried to echo in the line breaks of the poem that follows. I was remembering an incident from my childhood, interpreted anew from knowing the circumstances of my birth. I wanted the words to have a storytelling quality while having the rhythms of that time come through the line breaks and spaces to create a coherent and integrated moment.

The Milky Way

In my mother's bedroom, soft green wallpaper fronds
order a forest shade of warm, hushed by my parents' nightly dreaming.
Early fall frost cools the house, not frozen enough for coal
to be lit in the elephant furnace
                      silent in the cellar.

My father is in town at a seed plant meeting, leaving
my mother and me alone. The small shuttered
reading lamp burns above the pillows softly
as it does every night to soothe us into sleeping.

I've curled my arms to lock the nightgown below
the knees. My mother unbuttons her beige slacks, steps
out and kicks them to the chair. Her arms slide
from her threadbare cotton blouse, breasts falling open.

She adds her brassiere to the pile, slips on a long shirt, scoops
the clothes into the rocker by the old metal crib.
Her round smooth body brushes against flannel stretched
over her hips, her hands following last night's wrinkles.

Are you afraid of dying I ask, but she doesn't answer
sitting on the edge of the bed, brushing her hair.
Her eyes look past the hallway to the top of the stairs
as she listens
        settling sounds of the house.

I'm not, she says finally, because I've seen where dying goes
into the light and warm, a pathway to brilliance.
She points to the pale plaster ceiling, reaching her hands
for what I think must be the Milky Way.

I can hear in her voice that this is true and I return
to my bed, crawling beneath the goose down
wondering if this quiet darkness
is a doorway to the sky, the crescent moon

    spilt stars hum
    with the glow of my mother's reading lamp
    and the warmth of her body
    falling over the house
        like feathers.

                (Luce-Kapler, 2003, pp. 3–4)

In attending to language, either through poetry or otherwise,
the rhythm is an embodied experience. Lee explained that we become not just "self-contained subjects/observers;" rather we become embedded in kinaesthetic space. He wrote:

And when you register its frequencies, what configures you is both
outside you and within. You're a subset, a local constituent: one swatch
of the plural whole. Now subject and object unclench, subside to
secondary distinctions within the field. (p. 226)

Like Langer, Lee makes the biological connection, the connection between language, rhythm, and our lived experience. Writing poems involves one in the very heartbeat of remembering experiences and the cadence of existence where rhythm becomes an interpretation, a way of "reading" the world. The rhythms into which we are born and in which we live, such as our body cycles, comprise "a syntax for knowing." Rhythm reminds us that we are part of a complex world co-created by the human and the more-than-human in an ever unfolding, self-transcending relation.

Ezra Pound (1951) identified three primary forms of making poetic meaning—melopoeia (music), logopoeia (intellect), and phanopoeia (imagery)—that create a dynamic relationship within a poem. Molly Peacock (1999), in a similar vein, defined three systems in a poem: the line, the sentence, and the image that need to work together successfully. Within each of those systems are words with their particular stressed syllables. The lines and the sentence develop pauses, white space and breaks in the breathing. The image depends on the words, the lines, and the sentences, its evocative nature bringing depth and color to the poem's rhythm. Ideally, all these systems work together to bring us into a rhythmic moment of complexity. Within larger systems are nested smaller systems, each with its own rhythm that coemerges with other rhythms to become part of the larger system's measure of time (Briggs & Peat, 1999). In our reading of poetry, we can be attuned to the echoes of rhythm throughout the systems of a poem that create a coherent work.

Complexity theorists, in their investigations of living systems, explain how such systems self-organize to maintain an internal equilibrium while remaining open to the external environment. In creating larger systems, smaller systems will couple together, each with its own rhythm that co-emerges with other rhythms to become part of the larger system's measure of time (Briggs & Peat, 1999). In our reading of poetry, we can be attuned to the echoes of rhythm throughout the systems of a poem that create a coherent work.

The Rhythm of Writing

The importance of rhythm in writing first became a focus for me through my exploration of Emily Carr. In examining her art and reading her journals in preparation for writing a collection of poetry, I found references and images of rhythm in much of her writing and painting. Many times in her journal, Carr wrote about going into the woods and sitting, waiting for the thrum of the forest to begin. She sought the movement of living and then painted the cadences of such places.

As I "followed" her trail of cigarette smoke and the dribbles of paint across her studio floor, my understanding of the complexity of her life and relations began to unfold like the sweep of her brush across canvas. I came to know her more intensely than I could have imagined. This embodied knowing was a process of composing by juxtaposing my life to Emily's, by continuing a dialogue that created new images of my life and hers, and by reconciling how deeply interwoven our lives became through the rhythm of texts: paintings, stories and poems.

Maria Tippett, one of Emily's biographers, responded to a Carr painting in the following way:

> Like O'Keeffe, Emily did not paint the entire subject. She thrust her observer against the trunk, leaving the greatest portion of the cedar out of the painting. She attempted to imbue it with life and movement ... She juxtaposed light and dark colours, and achieved a rhythmic balance between the slowly curving ascending lines of the trunk and the falling draperies of the background foliage. (1979, p. 182)

Early on in the work, I felt this juxtaposition; there was no way of standing back and observing and speculating on Emily Carr's life without feeling mine bumped up against hers: Dark to light and light to dark. I stood silently before her paintings, caught up in the rhythms of those huge cedars; I spent time in the rainforest near Tofino, sitting in the depths of the woods, letting the thrum move me.

Alone among those trees I wrote:

Wait, Emily Carr says. Wait and things begin to move. I hear seedlings and dried leaves fall to the ground with a gentle crackling. A mosquito lights on my page, damp with humidity. I hear the wind in the upper reaches of the cedars. Evidence of its existence is in the sigh of movement and building crescendo. You can feel the burgeoning of life here, the breathing, expanding ground, the diminishing rot, the rich fecundity of old sinking, musty undertones shading green. Needles float onto the sleeve of my purple sweater. I hear the rising wind, the creaking of wood, a distant whistle and the far-off sound of the surf. No wonder Emily believed God was the spirit who moved through the forest.

Moving in close to Emily was not easy, however. As I continued to read her journals and stories, I grew impatient with her rhythms to the point where I would have to stop reading. I learned that this was a pattern of our relationship; I could not just read and nod my head. Emily challenged the difficult bits of my life, and this discomfort initiated some of the best dialogues, spanning a passion for artistic work to the demands placed upon a female artist. Her voice called me to pay attention to how the rhythm was forming my feeling. She wrote in her journal:

There is something additional, a breath that draws your breath into its breathing, a heartbeat that pounds on yours, a recognition of the oneness of all things. When you look at your own hand you are not conscious of feeling it (unless it hurts), yet it is all intimately connected up with us. Our life is passing through it. When you really think about your hand you begin to realize its connection, to sense the hum of your own being passing through it. (Carr, 1966, p. 215)

Through this deep engagement with Carr's work, my writing began to move from more distant and distinct dialogues to poems that embodied ideas through patterns of images and rhythms. I was beginning to reinterpret the cadences of a new relationship that shaped a different understanding such as in the following poem:

The Watchers

Far from lace curtains
that fragment her in rumours
her eyes cloud into forest
at the gray edge of weather

Shadowed crows clack their beaks
as she comes from underbrush
moss-covered and damp
grass stains on her knees
fir needles between her teeth

Into woods where spirits gather
murmuring totems and trees
their quiet blood whispers
through fronds and grasses
startling her gaze to paint

(Luce-Kapler, 2003, p. 36)

Working with the women writers further highlighted the importance of rhythm in the work of interpretation. With the young women, I searched for a way to understand the results of our coming together in a particular place where writing in response to various texts led to the gradual opening of interpretive possibilities in the young women's work.

The two breakthrough moments in the writing group, that is where the quality and subject of writing clearly shifted, occurred when Sidonie and I introduced two pieces of literature. When juxtaposing the writing to that literature, there was a clear echoing of the cadence, which seemed to create opportunities for the girls to reinterpret their experiences. The first event occurred during an in-group writing activity following the reading of a poem; the second happened when we sent the girls home with excerpts from Jeannette Winterson's essay, "The Semiotics of Sex" and asked them to write about "the forbidden."

In the first instance, Sidonie and I planned an activity that we hoped would move the girls past focusing on the dramatic and abstract themes to which teenagers gravitate, those of everlasting love, eternal betrayal, and deep sorrow. I began the session by reading "The Swimming Pool," a poem by Lorna Crozier, and asking everyone to write in response for fifteen minutes. Many of the pieces the girls wrote echoed Crozier's rhythms. The first few lines of the poem reflect the cadence of her work:

I used to be such
a swimmer, surface diving
to the loud blue hum around the grates,
following the lines and cracks
that led to a cave I could
never find the entrance to,
ears aching. All summer .... (1995, p. 62)

In response, Alexis wrote:

I could never
find a man
that moves with me
as water does. Is that wrong
water
it sends shivers of comfort
up my spine
not of ecstasy
of oneness

While the image of the water is repeated, the more powerful echo, it seems to me, is in the rhythm. Because Alexis only heard the poem, she had not followed Crozier's breaks; instead, she picked up some of the stresses and silence that she heard over several readings, choosing her own pauses and emphases to resemble the poem. Through following this pattern, Alexis developed a theme of asserting her autonomy and questioning the expectation that a man enhance her identity.

The second writing event began with a theme that arose continually during our group meetings—the notion of forbidden writing; i.e., "good girls don't write about sex," or "good girls don't write bad stuff." The young women were eager to try writing around that theme, but they were not clear about what we meant by "forbidden writing"; they had not thought of their earlier responses in that light. Sidonie suggested that we look at several pages of Winterson's, "The Semiotics of Sex," which takes on the issue of women writing the forbidden.

> How much can we imagine? The artist is an imaginer. The artist imagines the forbidden because to her it is not forbidden. If she is freer than other people it is the freedom of her single allegiance to her work. Most of us have divided loyalties, most of us have sold ourselves. The artist is not divided and she is not for sale. Her clarity of purpose protects her although it is her clarity of purpose that is most likely to irritate most people. We are not happy with obsessives, visionaries, which means, in effect, that we are not happy with artists. Why do we flee from feeling? Why do we celebrate those who lower us in the mire of their own making while we hound those who come to us with hands full of difficult beauty? (1995, p. 116)

Winterson's short direct sentences and her questions give this piece an insistence, a calling for the right to speak out, saying whatever one needs to say. When Sidonie read this aloud to the girls, we offered little explanation except to suggest they write their own "forbidden," and that they answer Winterson's call and say what they wished. We also suggested that they write in the third person, believing that this would give a small distance sometimes needed to write about strong emotions.

As with the Crozier piece, I could see where the insistent rhythm of Winterson's writing influenced the narratives of the girls and that this response was again "opening up" their writing to memories or feelings that they had not interpreted before in text.

Pegatha echoed Winterson's words and then picked up the rhythm to continue: "The artist is not divided and she is not for sale," she wrote. "She hides beneath, in the shell that has been created for her. She must create the crack which will give her the freedom she needs, wants, and deserves. The world around her forbids her to write, to express. It is considered childish and considered reaching for something that is not there."

Ayelha followed the short sentences and questioning of Winterson's style: "I remember being told, 'Curtsy like a princess with beautiful long hair. Don't play in the dirt. Wear the pretty and extravagant pink and white dresses. Couldn't play with the boys' toys. Here's a little purse and some make up.'" Then she asks: "What's going on? A marriage ring on both our fingers? I know where I am? These terrible words coming from my mouth? I know it's wrong but it seems to just flow."

Alexis, too, picks up on the short declarative sentences and the questions: "Her boyfriend confronts her. He cannot understand why she doesn't want to make out with him. After all they have been going out for three weeks and two days. Why does her body tense up? Why does she cringe whenever he gets close to her?"

While Winterson's words certainly challenged the girls to write whatever they wished, I was intrigued in the subtle adoption of the rhythmic style. Nearly every writer chose to use short declarative sentences and strong questions to give her writing an insistence that opened up the difficult events about which she wrote.

These two writing practices in the group, more than any others, changed the tenor of our working. In response to these activities, the girls became engaged in writing pieces that seemed more meaningful and important to them. They began to see this work as a way to challenge some of the expected roles with which they were struggling. An important impetus for this shift in their writing and interpretation I attribute to texts that engaged them in new rhythmical explorations as well as challenging discursive structures, such as Winterson's questions.

A few months after this writing group ended, Dennis Sumara and Brent Davis invited me to plan a culminating writing workshop for their research project with gay, lesbian, and transgendered teachers. Their study had engaged the participants in literary anthropological practices (Sumara, 2002) focusing on how such work might help them interpret the ways in which they negotiated minority identities within public school teaching. Sumara and Davis decided that some intensive work with writing was important because while the participants had learned strategies for negotiating their sexual identity positions within a largely heterosexist and homophobic culture of public schooling, they could not locate a language that represented the complexity of their insights.

My role would be leading a three-day writing workshop at an ocean retreat where the natural rhythms of the waves and rainforest replaced the urban rhythms by which the participants lived. To further draw attention to the rhythms about them, I used Virginia Woolf's novel, *The Waves*, as a guiding text. In her representation of the fluidity of consciousness, Woolf draws on the incessant, recurrent dips and crests of waves such as in her initial interlude:

> The sun had not yet risen. The sea was indistinguishable from the sky, except that the sea was slightly creased as if a cloth had wrinkles in it. Gradually as the sky whitened a dark line lay in the horizon dividing the sea from the sky and a grey cloth became barred with thick strokes moving, one after the other, beneath the surface, following each other, pursuing each other, perpetually.
>
> As they neared the shore each bar rose, heaped itself, broke and swept a thin veil of white water across the sand. The wave paused, and then drew out again, sighing like a sleeper whose breath comes and goes unconsciously. (1992, p. 3)

Drawing attention to the rhythm—both of the place and the texts—I invited the participants to write interpretive pieces that would focus on the environment and their bodily response to it. They had time to sit and wait for things "to slip into their places." Not only did writing require that individuals pay attention to their patterns of being in this location, such activity also included group readings and discussions where they had to attend to others' work. Listening to each other, writing in response and sharing insights meant that over the course of several days, a productive group rhythm emerged.

From the initial responses of the writers, the importance of inviting them to work in a place where the rhythms of the natural world were so insistent and present was clear. When asked to search for an object and prepare to tell a story about its finding, everyone chose to go outdoors. One listened to the waves and made a tape recording; another collected bark from a spruce covered in lichens; still another described the objects she found in a tidal pool. Many of them told how spending time in that space brought back memories of childhood or other visits or pleasant moments in their work. Within those moments of reflection, they had noticed how they were making connections across time and how the rich unfolding of relationships were recognized, acknowledging the entanglements of human and natural history. One woman wrote:

> I knew I was looking for Old Man's Beard before I left ... because the last time I was here I walked along the beaches and just picked it up off of the sand. I took it back to my classroom and last year my kids did a science fair and they dyed with these natural plants. So I knew I wanted to get some more off of the ground.... When you're going over the rocky head where you go through the trail parts there's always trees up there that Old Man's Beard is hanging off of or coating the branches. I always find it in places where it's really perfectly still and totally quiet.... It just feels really ancient to me, and really old. This can grow in amidst all this change and turmoil ... it grows so slowly and takes years and years.... It's just been there forever.

As the workshop progressed, their writings reflected a deepening sense of the interconnectedness of the human world with the non-human through the rhythmic attention echoing the cadences of the waves and the wind surrounding us. One woman wrote short phrases that reflected the lap of the waves:

> I breathe the sky. Stand in her. Heave my spirit in the trees. My body is an open current. My breath cooked air. From my mind's eye there

is no limit I tell you. The jade blue arches through conundrum leans into delft white court sky. The ocean snores fitfully. The milky tip-most tops of waves force the issue. Ghosts fold into one another becoming other. Pull me out of dream from Cat's Ear Creek to rainforest path. For spruce towers are great cathedrals. Rain faints. Hold fast to the vulnerable sky.

As with the Emily project and the work with the young women, this writing workshop revealed how important rhythm is to language and writing and how it becomes an interpretive tool for human experience. Further, the influence of the environment was clear in this latter work and brought to my attention that rhythm does not only come from our history of language usage or from the texts we read but also from the cadences of the natural world. As David Abram explained: "Language as a bodily phenomenon accrues to *all* expressive bodies, not just to the human. Our own speaking, then does not set us outside of the animate landscape but—whether or not we are aware of it—inscribes us more fully in its chattering, whispering, soundful depths" (1996, p. 80).

The Rhythm of Subjectivity

Language brings forth the sense of our selves, but while subjectivity is inherent in all expression, it can neither be controlled nor stabilized. As Jeannette Winterson wrote, "The self is not contained in any moment or any place, but it is only in the intersection of moment and place that the self might, for a moment, be seen vanishing through a door, which disappears at once" (1989, p. 80). Such a moment and place has a character that may emerge retrospectively in writing, the work becoming a medium to reveal traces of subjectivity as the writer describes an "I" who already is distinct from her or his material body. Through recognizing this other, Bakhtin (1981) explained, we find ourselves in mutual reflection and perception. The I who writes can trace some of the complicity, influences and possibilities in the I who is written about. It is this ability of language to "limn the actual, imagined and possible lives of its speakers, readers, writers" that gives it vitality (Morrison, 1993, p. 20).

Through the writing of those moments, we may strive to represent the particular rhythm of that time and space, or writing to a particular rhythm may lead us back to memories or toward emerging threads of our subjectivity. While the memories and experiences of our lives are multifaceted and ever-changing, human beings nevertheless struggle to realize unity in the unfolding of their lives, creating narratives about their selves to develop a pattern of identity (Kerby, 1991). While events are continually occurring to shift that story, over time coherence emerges so we do have a sense of ourselves or "who someone is."

In exploring Emily Carr's paintings and stories, I developed a sense of her rhythm that colored my poetry and surfaced memories that I interpreted in the new context, revealing my subjectivity at particular moments. In light of those insights, I had a different sense of who I had been and who I was becoming. This work brought an appreciation that our subjectivity cannot be shaped only through individual reflection, but rather, is a process of coming-to-be in relation to others.

The writing group with the young women emphasized how language is shared and ideas co-emerge with a group identity as subjectivities flow and merge into each other. The image that Flint uses in her reading of *The Waves* illuminates this process: "These divergent elements which make up the individual voices in *The Waves* are like the components of a tidal sea: the same molecules, in constant process of rearrangement, directed, like waves, by forces beyond themselves ..." (p. xxvi). While each piece of writing in the group was particular and individual, each revealed images and rhythms that drew it into the collective work of the group, each contributing to the coherence of the whole.

During the ocean workshop, for example, as participants shared and responded to writing, their consciousness of themselves in relation to the group heightened. Writing made possible such understandings because, as Olson (1994) explained, the emergence of writing enabled human beings to have an idea about an idea; that is, our consciousness of words created a distinction between the words themselves and the ideas they express. Such capabilities mean that humans can use written language as an object of reflection and analysis.

This workshop widened my understanding of the collective nature of rhythm and identity by moving beyond the group to include the surroundings and details that made up the context of the writing. The participants had the opportunity over several days to begin to follow the pattern of their thinking and recognize how engaging in a variety of experiences in a new interpretive location further shaped their identity. They listened to the natural rhythms of the ocean and rainforest, they responded in writing and through oral story, they created a group rhythm reflected in the work they did together, and they came away understanding their relationships to each other and to the world differently.

Writing about our experience means reflecting on lived moments that have passed; nevertheless, such reflection enables us to slow down the experience and notice its grounding. As Flint wrote, Virginia Woolf's desire in writing *The Waves* was to notice and investigate "her own patterns of thought, particularly when faced with the problem of understanding the nature of identity" (p. ix). As we investigate the patterns we may recognize how deeply entangled we are in the life forces of the world as we remember the susurration of waves or the sighing of the wind through a rainforest.

While the writing activities during the workshop enabled the participants to discover the relationships between their work as teachers and their sense of identity, it was when reading the transcripts that one could trace the relationship between identity and the broader contexts in which they emerge. For instance, one woman wrote:

> Pearl morning. A raucous caucus. I enter the earth mouth gorged with choice. Shades of grey splayed on her sandy tongue. Flies ricochet off my cheeks. I wave my hand over my face. Fingers spread in a circular motion like my mother when mosquitoes draw near .... Choose she who wails the loudest. Watch her rise. Wash her down. My child get-

ting ready for Sunday mass. Stone within stone within story within star. Cold against ear I hear the sea, the whole story. See it crease. Rumble through your viziers. Wrinkle your face. Shove coarse white light in places unprepared. Leaving you some 160 million years later pocked, scarred, scared. The taste of salty tears on your earlobe. Above exploding star, the redeeming stellar halo.

In their writing, the participants drew from their memories of being in the natural world threading them through their current experiences by the ocean, using them to interpret their lives and sense of identity.

Rhythms engage us in an interpretive experience whether in the midst of a writing group activity or deeply engaged with the work of a Canadian painter. Such a process, however, is not without its troublesome aspects. Confronting memories and issues through a different cadence opens our lives to a new rhythm. Engaging and interpreting with texts in this way changes our sense of subjectivity. "There is no going back," as one of the writer told me. Even so, involving ourselves in the interpretive possibilities of writing, gives a measure of being able to live more thoughtfully, aware of what the emerging patterns of our lives might be.

On the one hand, writing takes us away from our experience; we step back, we reflect on what has happened, we choose images and forms that we hope will convey to readers our understanding of that time. On the other hand, writing calls us to pay attention to the details, to the rhythms, and the shape of our living. We learn to notice the threads and hear the cadence in attending to the biological and phenomenological. Writing attunes us to our possible selves as we contribute to our emerging pattern of experience. Recognizing the role of rhythm in writing is important both for the creation of texts and for our reading of them. Rhythm reminds us of the embodiment of language, but also results from the social and cultural interpretations we bring to that language. In chapter 3, I investigate the effects of such a context.

chapter three

the language connection

Every good poem begins in language awake to its own connections—language that hears itself and what is around it, sees itself and what is around it, looks back at those who look into its gaze and knows more perhaps even than we do about who and what we are.

— Jane Hirshfield

On a shelf in my office, at about eye level, I have a cast of a woman's alabaster face. She emerges from a rock surface, her eyes large and still, a delicately shaped hand pressed against her lips. This woman has been my writing companion for many years, her face sometimes reflecting my struggle with words, my hesitation to speak, and my feelings of uncertainty about my ideas. Other times, I read her visage as one of contemplation and repose, reflecting deep intellectual moments. For me she embodies the tensions of being a woman who writes.

Several months ago, when a friend came to my office for the first time, she noticed the woman and remarked that the sculpture reminded her of a wall painting in her home country of Poland. This painting, an image of St. Anna created in the mid-8th century, shows a woman with a simple headdress, large eyes, and an index finger pressed against her lips. The expression and the pose are hauntingly similar to my sculpture.

Barbara Walker (1983) traces Saint Anne/Anna back to the early Goddess who people claimed to be the "Grandmother of God" and later considered the mother of Virgin Mary (p. 38). When the Catholic Church adopted Mary's immaculate conception as an article of faith in 1854, they also deemed St. Anne innocent of sexuality so that Mary could be born without the "taint of original sin" (p.

40). They later revised this dogma when two virgin births seemed one too many. The story suggested instead that Mary was freed of original sin while in the womb.

Looking at St. Anna's finger pressed against her lips, I wondered if she stopped an amused smile as the patriarchs argued about her possible sexual activities. Or perhaps she despaired that her subjectivity, the interpretation of her life, was once again taken from her. Her expression is enigmatic; I have no way of knowing what is behind those large still eyes, yet they remind me of the struggle women face in finding and saying the words to describe their experience as language brings with it a history of beliefs and contestation.

When I was a young girl and quite determined to be a writer, I was fortunate to be taught by some women who believed writing in a wide variety of forms should be encouraged through daily practice. Not until I reached high school did the opportunities for writing begin to narrow. There writing focused more on answers to questions and structured essays and it became clearer that the public realm did not necessarily deem my opinions and voice (or those of other women) important. This awareness was a gradual realization, an ephemeral process with no defining moment yet with a powerful effect. I began to doubt that what I was writing had value—intellectually or aesthetically. Even after years of writing, those old doubts still linger, and I see the uncertainty hovering beneath the writing of most woman with whom I have worked. Who gets to speak and whose words get the most space and recognition are important considerations. Nevertheless, while language often conceals these processes of power, it also has the energy to work in ways that are generative and creative and become its own source of power.

One of the young women from the writing group exemplified this potential for writing to reveal both language's constraints and creative possibilities. Alexis, with great courage, wrote about an incident that had happened to her when she was eight years old. A twelve-year-old neighbor boy had encouraged her to engage in a supposedly innocent exploration of her body that ended up leaving her feeling violated. Alexis struggled with the ambivalence she felt about the event, on the one hand denying that it had been a terrible experience for her and on the other hand using language that revealed the depth of her discomfort. Using third person, she wrote: "He is nice, she thought, he put his jacket down for me so I would not get dirty ... She looks back now and realizes he was probably covering his own ass."

After reading, Alexis explained that the incident had not made her feel bad, but that writing and talking about it so that other people became part of the experience, was difficult for her. She continually insisted, too, that we should not think that "all guys were this way," even to the point where she wrote a postscript about a boyfriend who hears the story and understands. She ends with the lines: "And so she says to him, not this boy, this boy is hope. He holds her in his arms and kisses her gently. This boy *is* hope. He is reassurance that some men in the world are safe. With his tears she would finally forget."

Alexis struggled to work through the feelings—writing partly as "good girls should" but also wondering what this experience meant for her. The narrative opened up some of the feelings she had about this incident but also revealed how Alexis read the cultural construction of women and sexuality.

When I interviewed Alexis at the end of the writing group, she told me that exploring such experiences through writing had helped her to be braver in her expression of what she was feeling and thinking. She seemed less concerned about the expectations for her as evidenced by the play she had written for a teenage festival. The story explored the dimensions of relationship through various scenarios, including a lesbian love scene. "I don't really care what people think anymore," she said. Although I suspected this was not entirely true, she still expressed a confidence far beyond that with which she had begun the group.

Another member of the group and her collaborator in the play recalled the discussion about the scene: "I just remember us saying 'let's do a lesbian scene,' Pegatha said. 'It will be so funny.' And then we're talking about it and then I remember eventually saying, 'Well, why couldn't we? It ties in with everything. It's not that big of a deal. It's not like we're going to have sex on stage or anything.' And then it was just like we were 'hey if we wrote it and worded everything correctly and got the right actresses to do it then it could work'."

The girls initially broached the topic of a lesbian scene with giggling discomfort, but once the idea was spoken, they began to consider it seriously and Alexis worked to write a credible scene in spite of some opposition from adults in the community. Through the opportunity to write in a group and talk about that writing, Alexis developed an appreciation for the potential power of her words and the possibilities for expression.

When I was in high school, I had one opportunity to really explore writing through a course called "Language 21" that was an option for those who wanted to experience the demands and skills of writing fiction and poetry. Although our teacher did not offer her own work, we had a sense that she too was a writer just by the way she spoke about the process and the serious responses she gave our pieces. Her air of familiarity and passion for the craft gave a real legitimacy to our work. I remember this class not only to note how this was my first important exposure to working with a group of writers, but also to recall one of the stories that I wrote and how it revealed similar struggles to that of Alexis in her writing.

The story is a science fiction piece about three women astronauts who have the opportunity to go the moon. I carefully described their capabilities, making it clear that they were more than qualified to be going to the moon. In reading this work now, I smile at the obvious way I constructed the women's experience based on the feminist discourses of the day. It is the ending, though, that startles me. Just as the women are to land, things begin to go horribly wrong and it seems that they are not able to cope after all. The final scene, as they are blown into oblivion, suggests that this was because they were women.

Today, I am appalled by that ending and at the time, apparently, so was my teacher. She wrote in the margin: "Whose side are you on anyway?" Good question. And it was good because here was an adult woman responding to my work in a way that made me take notice of what I had written. Without even recognizing it, I had succumbed to the ambivalence toward feminist values with which so many young women like Alexis struggle. Both writing events, occurring twenty-six years apart, reveal the difficulty of writing about women in a way that does not replicate patriarchal constructions. They show how powerfully those beliefs are constructed and reinforced and how difficult they are to denaturalize.

These writing events and others like them were my impetus for investigating how such engagements with language can be revelatory and transforming. This chapter considers how particular writing practices are important occasions for learning and understanding as we work to shape language with our own intentions, beginning with feminist theorists who have examined women's relationship to language and then relating those ideas to the work of Bakhtin. Near the end of the chapter, I take the opportunity to reread a transcript to show how our understandings change over time and to illustrate how one can read the traces of influence in texts.

Women and the Symbolic Order

Many women have written about the constraints of language, including exploring some of the mythical and historical roots of such control. Two examples are Laurie Finke's study of medieval female mystics and Luce Irigaray's reading of Plato's cave myth.

Finke (1992), in her examination of feminist theory through women's writing, described how, during the Middle Ages, the church constricted the female role in spiritual life and religious work until women were effectively cloistered in religious orders. Some of those women responded, however, by claiming mystical experiences and by relaying words inspired by God, which served to open up space to speak within a patriarchal and misogynistic society. While some of these mystics engaged in extreme self-punishing measures— including flagellation and starvation—they nevertheless found a way to enter into the public discourse.

Finke explained that medieval Christianity construed men as spirit and women as body and, since religion was the dominant mode of expression in that society, this thinking had considerable impact. Mysticism became a way for women such as Saint Leoba, Margery Kempe and Angela of Foligno to stretch those bounds and to turn the dominant discourse to their own purposes. "The discourse of the female mystic was constructed out of disciplines designed to regulate the female body and it is, paradoxically, through these disciplines that the mystic consolidated her power" (Finke, p.78).

Finke described these practices as "poaching," a term used by Michel de Certeau to identify the strategies that "parasitically undermine hegemonic cultural practices and enable the disempowered to manipulate the conditions of their existence" (p.10). Such strategies deflect the power of the social order without challenging it overtly. The visions of the mystics served to free them from conventional roles assigned to women, created opportunities for them to be genuine religious figures and gave them a public language that could even attack injustice within the church. While the mystics could and did subvert clerical authority, the Church also strictly defined and controlled the nature and content of the mystical experience by cloistering them in a setting that structured life through the liturgy and rituals. Nevertheless, Finke suggested that the "mystic's pain—her inflicting of wounds upon herself—allows her to poach upon the authority of both Church and state, enabling her to speak and be heard, to have followers, to act as a spiritual adviser, to heal the sick, and to found convents and hospitals" (p. 95).

Luce Irigaray, using psychoanalysis as a framework, explored the struggle of women to find a place of speaking in the symbolic order where the discourse of femininity and maternity allows patriarchy to cover over the experience of women and mothers. From Irigaray's perspective, women have been represented only in comparison to men. Thus they are seen as a lack, the opposite, or the complement of the male subject and, according to the symbolic order, do not exist in their own right.

Irigaray traced the source of this exclusion to Plato's myth in which he described the cave as a womb where Socrates, acting as midwife, used these maieutic methods to assist into birth the knowledge of truth. Irigaray understands this story as a fantasized copulation between the mother and father that attempts to remove the mother. "The effect is that the male function takes over and incorporates all the female function, leaving women outside the scene, but supporting it, a condition of representation" (Whitford, 1991b, p.106).

Plato's analogy progresses from the dark cavern where reflections and echoes of the world flicker to the world itself and then beyond to the realm of Ideas and truth. In three scenes, the cave (Mother) is separated from Ideas (Father) with no possibility of commingling since the world fills the middle space and prevents their intercourse. For change in the symbolic order to occur, Luce Irigaray explained that women must be able to speak their identity, to speak as women within that order.

A short story by Italo Calvino (1989) helps to illustrate the mythical implications of the cave for men and women. In "The Adventure of a Poet," the characters, Usnelli, a "fairly well-known poet," and Delia H., "a very beautiful woman" approach an island in a rubber canoe. As they draw near the island, Usnelli comments on the silence. He hears the babble of its world—the rustle of vegetation, animal calls, bird wings—but can discern no meaning. Delia revels in this world as she lies in the boat speaking with "constant ecstasy about everything she was seeing" (p. 103) while Usnelli tries to push away the sensations. "He, distrustful (by nature and through his literary education) of emotions and words already the property of others, accustomed more to discovering hidden and spurious beauties than those that were evident and indisputable, was still nervous and tense" (p. 104). For Usnelli, every flash of blue water or shadow of a fish's fin, points to something higher, farther away, "a different planet or new word" (p.104).

They paddle into a grotto that begins as a spacious, interior lake, but soon becomes a narrow dark passage. Usnelli watches the reflecting light and sees:

> The light from outside, through the jagged aperture, dazzled with colors made more vivid by the contrast. The water, there, sparkled, and

> the shafts of light ricocheted upwards, in conflict with the soft shadows that spread from the rear. Reflections and glints communicated also to the rock walls and the vault the instability of the water. (p. 104)

He finds that he is speechless, nervous, and unable to translate any of his sensations into words while Delia calls out and discovers with delight the echo. The cave becomes a creative power for her even as it robs Usnelli of his linguistic prowess.

As they continue, the darkness deepens along with Usnelli's fear and confusion of the unknown and strange feelings that also finally silence Delia. They agree to turn back, aborting their journey and returning to the edge of the cave where it opens onto the sea. They linger at this boundary while Delia goes for a swim. As she moves through the water where Usnelli can see her, she returns to being a fantasy creature for him: "her body at times seemed white (as if that light stripped it of any color of its own) and sometimes as blue as that screen of water" (p. 105). Delia's function for Usnelli becomes one of representing that which is outside discourse. In watching her, Usnelli realizes that what he is seeing is beyond language:

> He understood that what life now gave him was something not everyone has the privilege of looking at, open-eyed, as at the most dazzling core of the sun. And in the core of this sun was silence. Nothing that was there at this moment could be translated into anything else, perhaps not even into memory. (p. 106)

The arrival of some local fishermen interrupts Delia's water dance and serves to break the spell of the cavern. Delia and Usnelli are back in the world with its smells, noises, and earthiness. While Delia speaks to the fisherman, Usnelli remains silent: "this anguish of the human world was the contrary to what the beauty of nature had been communicating to him a little earlier: there every word failed, while here there was a turmoil of words that crowded into his mind" (p. 107). The noise, confusion and sensations of the fishing village bombard Usnelli. He realizes that there is no returning to his realm of poetic ideals, that by traveling to the cave, he has lost the orderly distance of language until "only the black remained, the most total black, impenetrable, desperate as a scream" (p. 108). There is nothing productive or reproductive possible; the intercourse between the mother and father is prevented because the world intervenes between the earthy, sensual darkness of the cave and the brilliant realm of Ideas. The father-poet can no longer produce or reproduce. He is impotent.

Usnelli represents the patriarchal fear of a return to the cave as well as a desire to do so. The threat is one of a loss of language and reason for men and a regaining of women's position in the symbolic order. Patriarchy desires to take over the cave for its own ends, for it to be a place of appropriation and until it is able to do so, the cave remains a fearsome place of darkness and chaos. In Calvino's tale this fear and desire is played out through the male poet while the reader is left speculating about Delia still chatting with the local inhabitants amidst their dried reddish seaweed and gasping fish.

In her consideration of women's aesthetic practices, Rita Felski believes that while the symbolic order essentializes women and inscribes them into patriarchy through language, she warned against seeing women as entirely determined by and excluded from a repressive "male" language. To do so, she suggested, is to ignore "the flexible, innovative, and creative capacities of language itself and particular instances of richness and complexity of women's language use ..." (1989, p. 62).

Thinking of Calvino's story from this perspective, then, a tale told from Delia's point of view might well feature the cave as an inviting place to visit rather than a metaphor of fear and, as for many women writers, become a place to re-imagine and to be creatively energized rather than traumatized. Gilbert and Guber, in their examination of women's representation in literature, explained the richness of this metaphor:

> Where the traditional male hero makes his 'night sea journey' to the center of the earth, the bottom of the mere, the belly of the whale, to

slay or be slain by the dragons of darkness, the female artist makes her journey into what Adrienne Rich has called 'the cratered night of female memory' to revitalize the darkness, to retrieve what has been lost, to regenerate, reconceive, and give birth. (1979, p. 99)

Patricia Yaeger discovered such a journey in Mary Oliver's poem "Mussels." The poem is set in the deeps, in a cave that is dangerous and yet salt-refreshed; a place where the narrator gathers the negative metaphoric potential of the cave, condenses and consumes it so that positive mythic possibilities can be re-envisioned. "Oliver's narrator is someone who both *is* the cave and is *in* it," Yaeger wrote, "who can move freely about exploring its chthonic powers before returning to the surface to berate and rename this space's negative meaning" (1988, p. 131).

Well before I considered the image of the cave as an important metaphor for women, I chose one of my favorite poems by Lorna Crozier mentioned in the second chapter. It so happens that this piece has a narrator who searches for the entrance to a cave in a swimming pool, which she never finds, but through the search becomes covered in a "birth-gleam" that accompanies an inability to speak, her mouth compared to an anemone opening and closing. The water, which seemingly springs from the cave, births her into sexuality, an experience for which she has no words. When the narrator swims at night, a strange boy joins her and they explore each other's bodies silently in the darkness. The sense of metamorphosis in this poem cannot happen through language, but only through this physical exploration bathed in water with a boy who may or may not really exist. The narrator speaks with a sense of fantasy that makes the whole experience seem mystical and often beyond language. One of the girls, Ayelha, wrote a response to the poem that is strangely reminiscent of Calvino's story:

Eyes bright and blue like the pools of the sea. Blue like the sky at the birth of spring, soft, delicate and clear. Through the forest, darkness comes about. As I walk along the soft dirt path, the thundering sound of leaves crunches beneath my feet. The sound leads me to a pitch black cave. My heart is breaking in remembrance of the boy I met that day. Crawling on my hands and knees, I enter the warm and protected cave. The summer fresh air enters my lungs it feels so cold. I look up and realize that the earth around me is spinning. I force a sound from my mouth but I am at a loss for words. I notice some small clumps of grass near the entrance of the cave. The sharp blades tickle my soft hands, happiness overcomes my fear. The night is rapidly approaching. Cool winds send me running out of the forest. The moonlight guides my way. I hear faint whispers as I run. For a brief moment I feel the presence of the boy I truly love, but it turned out to be the wind whipping by. Coming out of the forest leaves me unprotected. I feel the wings of the mothering bird let me go. Sadly my eyes fill with tears, they fall like perfect raindrops from the sky. Smashing into my hands with an echoing sadness. I tumble to my knees in the blackness of the night.

Like Delia and Usnelli, the narrator moves from light into darkness as she enters the cave. However, while Delia found a voice in the cave, this young woman is speechless, her senses heightened by what she discovers there. She has come to the cave to find some way of connecting with a boy she has met, but finds that such a thing cannot happen in this place. The cave leaves her almost breathless and feeling trapped. Cool winds send her away from the cave, reborn as she runs through the dark forest until she is left outside the protection (and danger) of the cave, alone and lonely in the awareness that her dreams of a relationship are unrealized. Even so, she believes the cave to be a place of warmth and protection, a touchstone, home ground.

As Gilbert and Gubar explained and as the writing of Mary Oliver and Ayelha illustrate, language is not all encompassing in its representation. While it is socially constructed in ways that try to limit meaning, there are cracks and crannies from which other possibilities and new understanding emerge. Elizabeth Grosz related this potential for alternative understandings to feminist theory. She suggested that feminism needs to understand subjects not as "powerless, oppressed, furtive or defeated, nor as self-contained and pregiven agents, but as operative vectors, points of force, lines of movement, resistance or complacency, subjects who function strategically, and actively, within power networks which are unable to 'rob' them of agency or activity" (2000, p. 2).

She explained that the very existence of feminist thought would not be possible were it not for the ability to imagine and move beyond subordination and domination. This is not to suggest that oppression and exclusion of women is non-existent, rather it is to point out the presence of avenues that may offer a different understanding and that may forge different pathways to power. Grosz interpreted the work of Irigaray as pointing to how this process might occur:

> Irigaray's questions are thus not questions about what to do, how to act, how to write in such a way as to be faithful to the lives and experiences of 'real women,' ... how to develop conceptual schemas, frameworks, systems that reveal what is at stake in dominant representational systems, and how to develop different ways of theorizing, based on the recognition of what has been left out of those dominant models. In other words, how to think, write or read *not* as a woman, but more complexly and less clearly, how to think, write and read otherwise, whether one is a man or a woman, how to accommodate issues, qualities, concepts that have not had their time before. (p. 18)

Grosz explained how we have infinite pasts available to us and that we can interpret and re-interpret those pasts without ever exhausting them. The interpretation of the past in the present is what shapes the future. To create a future of different representational possibilities, writers can develop a sensitivity to their language, questioning its history and character and search for places to subvert the expected and reconceptualize the familiar.

To begin identifying how such possibilities exist in language, a useful starting point is the theoretical work of Mikhail Bakhtin who identified the interplay of social forces and language.

The Heteroglossia

Writing is an immersion into a sea of language whose meanings and character intertwine with the diversity of human understanding and the rhythm of our existence. As an engagement with language, writing becomes part of that larger system, a system that reveals traces of interconnection in every word, what Bakhtin (1981) called the "heteroglossia." He described how language comes to us with the flavor of its previous interactions crystallized in what he called speech genres—"the residue of past behavior, an accretion that shapes, guides, and constrains future behavior" (Morson & Emerson, 1990, p. 290). While we depend on these speech genres, we also use their resources for new purposes that express our intentions in a refracted way.

Bakhtin defined such language use as utterances, which he distinguished from sentences by suggesting that the latter are infinitely repeatable, a form rather than something said while the former occur in a specific context that is not repeated. The context of an utterance arises from the histories of those words, from the stand the speaker or writer has chosen to take in relation to those words, and from her awareness of a real or imagined listener or reader of that utterance. We shape our utterances for our own intentions even while our words are drawn from the heteroglossia with its diversity of histories.

The heteroglossia is a wonderful amalgam of threads from which speakers and writers draw. These different threads of a language, including formal usage, slang, jargon, and dialects among others, are colored by the specific ways in which they have been conceptualized, understood and evaluated. Language is shaded with a complexity of experience, ideas, and attitudes knitted together. Bakhtin described it as thus:

> The word ... enters a dialogically agitated and tension-filled environment of alien words, value judgments and accents, weaves in and out of complex interrelationships, merges with some, recoils from others, intersects with yet a third group: and all this may crucially shape dis-

course, may leave a trace in all its semantic layers, may complicate its expression and influence its entire stylistic profile. (1981, p. 276)

Heteroglossia has a dynamic tension between centripetal forces where multiple possibilities come together in a desire for a unitary language and the centrifugal forces which destabilize those possibilities and stratify language: construction and destruction at the same time.

To get a sense of this dynamic process, one need only imagine the heteroglossia of a school where external educational discourses from Ministries, the public and media exert pressure on teachers to define and speak of learning in particular ways while teachers struggle against this generalized and often dehumanizing language to remember the particular students in their classes. Within the school the discourses of discipline seek to mold students in particular directions while students develop their own language that questions this authority and pressures for space to define themselves on their own terms. One could think of many more examples within a school setting or many other locations where the struggles for power and language are evident.

In their description of heteroglossia, Morson and Emerson noted: "Such is the fleeting language of a day, of an epoch, a social group, a genre, a school, and so forth. It is possible to give a concrete and detailed analysis of any utterance, once having exposed it as a contradiction-ridden, tension-filled unity of two embattled tendencies in the life of language" (1990, p. 272).

When relating Bakhtin's description of language to writing, we can see that like oral language, writing is not solely the public production of a fixed text but rather a "dynamic meeting of reflection and production: a complex and ongoing interplay among personal and public voices" (Welch, 1993, p. 3). The history of meaning associated with words and the shared rhythms of language are part of a writer's work as she attempts to shape that language and engage some of her own history in its use, struggling against the forces that would narrow interpretation and exclude women.

Karen Hohne and Helen Wussow suggested developing a feminist dialogics from Bakhtin's work that describes feminine *êtres* (to be) rather than a feminine *écriture* (writing). By this they mean a way of living, an ethic as well as an epistemology, which considers the struggle between socio-linguistic points of view. "Feminine *êtres* would emphasize the relationships between race, class, gender, time, and space, rather than simply the multiplicity of voices and strategies for utterance through which women make themselves heard" (1994, p. xiv).

Rather than just realizing the dialogic possibilities for women's voices, then, feminine *êtres* suggest the need for critique and analysis, for exploring and describing the contexts in which the language is found. To begin to explore the alternative pasts of which Grosz speaks in order to reinterpret them toward a different future, it is important for women to consider the cultural, social and historical shaping of language. Through a more critical awareness of these forces, they can both understand and interrupt some of its influences.

In an early interpretation of one of the sessions from the teachers' writing group, I created a structure for critiquing and analysing a transcript (Luce-Kapler, 1997b). I was dissatisfied with the ways of representing research that were commonly available. I felt that block chunks of transcribed conversations placed within the texts did not reveal the rhythm and vitality of my participants' words. Some of the interpretations that were possible in listening to them were no longer possible in such a static format.

I began by returning to the tapes and listening to the conversation as I read along with the transcript. As I listened, I began marking the written text with slashes, similar to line breaks for a poem. I turned off the tape recorder and re-typed the transcript into a poetic form, not changing words, but creating lines. As I did so, I realized different interpretations were emerging from the text, but I was not sure how to interpret all that might be possible.

In my search for alternatives in my analysis, I discovered three categories suggested by Usher and Edwards: con-text, pre-text, and sub-text (1994, p.153). They suggested the importance of acknowledging reflexivity in educational research, which considers how researchers are *part of* rather than *apart* from the world they research. Being aware that the operation of reflexivity goes beyond the personal, they noted, one should reveal the place of power and discourse in the research text.

The framework which they proposed for interrogating textuality and foregrounding reflexivity in the writing and reading of research texts draws on Derrida's notion of the " 'general' text which subsumes but goes beyond specific texts" (p. 153); that is, that the boundaries of texts are fluid as I described in the preface. Con-text (with the text) considers the situatedness of the researcher/reader, including embodiedness and embeddedness. Pre-text (before the text) attends to the language and signification, binary oppositions, writing and textual strategies, as well as the cultural and interpretive traditions within which the research occurs. Sub-text (beneath the text) examines the professional paradigms, discourses, and power-knowledge formations at work.

In what follows, I revisit a research story that I first read using the structures explained above. I chose to return to a former text rather than working with a new piece because I want to draw on that earlier reading and look specifically at how interpretations change with time and how an earlier interpretation affects this reading. Such a process exemplifies for me Grosz's suggestion that there are infinite pasts available for us to understand.

Opening Up the Text

Transcripts pose a difficulty for me. Too often they are quoted like chunks of text from a book as if there were no bodies in that room speaking to each other, shuffling pages, moving into the writing with hesitance. I wonder in looking at the pages of transcription where this event took place. Was it on someone's back deck in the middle of summer? Was it a grey day in November? I want to visualize the writers, imagine what they are thinking as they begin to read their poems or their stories, so I set the scene of this transcript, realizing that this is my interpretation and that the other two women might have noticed the light falling across the sofa in quite a different way. One, after a difficult afternoon of teaching, might see the clouds gathering outside the living room window. Another, anticipating an evening of singing with her partner, might observe that the violets on the end table are blooming.

I have a memory of two friends, who are also writers and teachers, on a chilly February afternoon. I had turned the heat up so it was warm and pulled the easy chair close to the coffee table across from the sofa so we were in this comfortable circle. This is my story, my interpretation of this time as I sat across from two women with a maple coffee table, a pot of raspberry tea, and a plate of oatmeal cookies between us. The words were woven among us three through gesture, smile, giggle, guffaw, a wave of the hand, a passing of paper, a pouring of tea, a downturn of the eyes, a toss of the head, a listening.

I am conscious that research may be a subtle form of writing the self in ways that engage others. I continue to believe that about research, that we explore what we want to know to help us understand our place in the world. And if we do it well, others can read our texts and understand themselves in turn. The writer initiates the research, creates the space and becomes implicated. The research bespeaks her as she bespeaks the research.

Later, hearing the tape through muffled headphones there are only disembodied voices and hollow laughter, but it is enough to return memory to the room where there are the three of us: three become dimension; three-dimensional. As a raspberry bush blooms from the teapot, I watch the berries thicken, drip red juice. The reverberations of memory are the folds of sensory detail woven in that room.

When I reread the transcripts, however, typed from the tapes, the voices seem silenced; the page dead. There is no space for the reader to take a sip of tea, to laugh where the text reads [General laughter], to sigh at the [Long pause]. I wonder about writing a story, just a short fictional reconstruction, which will invite readers to be present in that room, taste the oatmeal cookies and see the snow blowing outside the window. I am fearful, though, of that authorial voice that seems to emerge when I write fiction and that has no hesitation in stepping inside characters, feeling what they feel and taking liberties. Such commingling seems invasive and disrespectful of those who did not live wholly in my imagination.

I think instead of writing poetry where I search for the pattern in my perceptions, sensations and emotions. What is the thread that I can follow through the circle of women, the rhythm of their words, the light of late winter, and the end of a long day of teaching? That thread begins to draw sensation together into a center of gravity that is a revelation of that time. A revelation but not *the* revelation. The words, the sounds, the patterns become the impetus for sense-making rather than a confusion of moments. How things are said matters as much as what is said. A poem filled with profound images falters if it is carelessly constructed. There is possibility in poetry for shaping the words of a research transcript, of revitalizing them. The researcher does not create new language, but reveals her interpretation of those words through rhythm, juxtaposition, and placement on the page. A page where a "pause" is not written but enacted, where laughter unfolds from the break in the line, the speed of the phrase, the space left for the reader. Writing the transcript as poetry invites hidden aspects and creates the unexpected.

Research Re-textured

THREE WOMEN SEARCH FOR TIME TO WRITE

I do more writing, but in snatches.
Caroline says to me
you have to put aside
      Caroline in her way says
you have to put aside half an hour everyday
or one hour everyday

and then I'm:
putting aside one hour to find time to go for a walk,
to find time for a nap,
to find time to read a book so I'm ready
for what I'm doing tomorrow
and there's so many hours
                I put aside
I don't have anymore hours for writing.

So what happens is that I get invited to something
and I don't have anything new
so I'm pressed for time and I whip something up.
Which isn't bad because
I work okay under deadline but
this takes more time
This takes crafting.
The deadline.

          I agree. I can't—I can't
          just sit like I couldn't
          just sit down last night
          and write something
          for today
          because I just had too many other
          things
          going on in my head
          and it's not,
          it's not my real writing,
          it's not real.
          I don't know.

I had only minutes to write
    I like some of those pieces,
    but they are really
    bereft of imagery.

    I think anyway.

this year
I've had time to spend with Emily.
So I think what you're saying
about time is really
an important thing.
That being able to be there
and yet I mean I've struggled
with this for so long—
how to find the time and still live
and—

raise a family and—

I don't know. I just don't know
how to do all the things. I
don't know. I just
don't know
how to do it very well. Sometimes
there's little windows
like right now for me
where I can do it,
but I know this won't last.

So how can
I guess you learn to write
under those constraints.
I mean—look—
out of incredible horrible circumstances,
great literature is born
but my god.

Con-text: With the Text

As writer and first reader of this research text, I begin by interrogating my situatedness, my embodiedment in the text. I am there like I was in that room in February. The feel of upholstery beneath my fingers, thick wool socks resting on the edge of the table, the weight of pages settled on my lap. They rustle and I hear my life in earlier writing groups hovering on the edges. A radio show about women that I heard last night while driving home is not far from awareness, and the edginess from yesterday's poetry class is still evident in the way I hug my poem to my chest. Voices of others intertwine with mine as I speak about the story one of the women just read to us; they color my thinking.

Rereading the transcript poem I remember my edge of desperation to find space to write. Not just then but earlier when my children were small and I had resolved to stay at home with them and become a writer. Two small children who shunned naps and seemed always busy exploring the nooks and crannies of our small house did not allow much time for quiet, for reflection and contemplation. The words moved from my typewriter with excruciating slowness. Now that my children are grown, however, I still find it difficult to make it to my computer to spend the hours writing that I imagine I desire. So time and quiet perhaps are only part of the issue.

Why is it so difficult to be a teacher and writer? Certainly obligations do influence the possibilities. There also is the awareness that when I write, I have to face who I am, what I know and what I do not. I cannot depend on someone else's words to see me through as I can when reading a book. I have to squarely face the possibility that I may not be able to say what I feel most deeply, or I may not want to see how my thinking and by extension, myself, emerge from the page. There is something raw about this kind of work that is both enticing and terrifying.

I recognize, too, that there is some privilege in this angst. That because I am white and middle-class with a job that values writing, I can express this uncertainty, take chances with my doubts, and test the waters. The three of us in the living room are fortunate in many ways and always hovering about the edges of our conversations about writing are the voices of women less so.

My experience as a writer, as a poet cannot be banished from this research. I hear the rhythms of the women's voices and imagine a poem; the images of women writing, of women desiring writing, color my interpretations. My writing is the research; the research the writing.

When I bring this poetic rendition of our conversation to the women in the group, they are excited about what I heard. They resolve to take pieces of the transcript themselves and interpret our words through their own rhythms from their perspective.

Later that year, the three of us perform a play that arises from this work: Sidonie has written a song; Casey choreographs a dance; we shape the words into a dramatic reading. The performance reinterprets our conversations, brings many facets to the work that began in that living room in February.

Pre-text: Before the Text

In tracing the threads that contributed to our conversation that afternoon, I think about how the text arises from a tangle of voices, texts, textual strategies and interpretations all shaded with social and cultural significance. We see ourselves connected to the history of women writers who have struggled for space in a literary world that privileged the male voice. The perspective of John Gardner is representative of many such opinions as he confesses that his wife Joan has imaginative suggestions for his characters and she really should be considered a collaborator: "I use a lot of people, Joan in particular. She hasn't actually written many lines because Joan's too lazy for that. But she's willing to answer questions. The extent of her contributions doesn't quite approach collaboration in the modern sense" (cited in Olsen, 1978, p. 222).

I want to hear Joan's side of the story. The tale of women's intellectual and creative contributions being diminished, sidelined, or hidden is not an unusual one. What we have valorized as great writing, as "real" literature, has been a particular way of seeing and responding to the world. And written mostly by men who feel that to create great art is to withdraw from the world into garrets and ivory towers and to use the language of the father tongue that creates gaps and distance between the experience of relationship and the word.

> A man finds it (relatively) easy to assert his 'right' to be free of relationships and dependents, à la Gauguin, while women are not granted and do not grant one another any such right, preferring to live as part of an intense and complex network in which freedom is arrived at, if at all, mutually. Coming at the matter from this angle, one can see why there are no or very few 'Great Artists' among women, when the 'Great Artist' is defined as inherently superior to and not responsible towards other. (LeGuin, 1989, p. 231)

Those are the conditions for women writing within patriarchal definition. Adrienne Rich calls for the need to re-vision women's writing. It is a matter of survival, she said, that we see with fresh eyes and enter the old text in a critical new direction. "Until we can understand the assumptions in which we are drenched we cannot know ourselves" (1979, p. 43). Reading the transcript of our conversations about writing, I can see some of the assumptions we bring to why we write—or do not write. As well as the reverence and desire tangled through our words, we feel the weight of the roles that have been put upon us and that we have, many times, unconsciously adopted.

Re-visioning women's writing begins by understanding that "women's writing" is not to be understood as one aesthetic practice or form. As Grosz suggested, we need to move away from feminist approaches that speak of "women's writing" or "writing like a woman" where "women or femininity was understood as self-contained, given identities, unique, different from men, oppressed and victimized subjects who were powerless" (2000, p. 2). It is important to recognize how women have not had their own place, a sex which is not one, as Irigaray says, and understand how the patriarchy has defined the feminine in roles to support its identifications. At the same time, however, we can work towards imagining and writing otherwise.

Is the struggle for time and the desire to write revealed in the research text saying more? Is there a desire to find space to write about experience in a world that still has walls that try to narrow women's possibilities?

> it's not my real writing
> how to find the time and still live and

raise a family
> I just don't know how to do it very well

Perhaps that is why the poetry is important for this interpretation. It reopens space and has room for questions to echo. Poetry can threaten the organization of the symbolic order and the stability of meaning in its silences, in its spaces that speak as loudly as words. In our writing, in our conversations about that work, we need to listen to the silences as much as the flurry of language about our busyness and our preoccupation with our daily obligations. Perhaps the silences can help us think about where those demands may be coming from and how we can respond otherwise.

Chris Weedon described such possibility in language referring to Kristeva's conception of the "semiotic chora"—those aspects of language that go beyond consciousness and the symbolic order. When an individual enters the symbolic order, there is a process of repression, which seeks to create a unitary subject (a centripetal force); however, the process is challenged through semiotic generation (a centrifugal force). This semiotic chora "is manifest in symbolic discourse in such aspects of language as rhythm and intonation and is at its strongest in non-rational discourses which threaten the organization of the symbolic order and the stability of its meanings, such as poetry, art and religion" (1987, p. 89). We bring our own meanings, our own rhythms to the language of our experience even though those words are colored by other experiences. As such, it is at the level of subjectivity where meaning is created, meaning that can disrupt the rational and linear interpretation of the world.

Sub-text: Beneath the Text

I envisage putting my ear to the line. Listening to those gaps, waiting in the silences. There are echoes below the text of multiple voices, multiple discourses. And other texts called and recalled. The intertextuality shadows, hovers and sometimes illuminates. Underneath every line of the research text, voices speak about what we should and should not do, who we are and are not. In listening, though, one recognizes a measure of choice and begins thinking of how to interrupt, how to resist.

Virginia Woolf claims that there is no more subversive act than writing from a woman's experience of life using a woman's judgment. Such writing is difficult. If we are too aware of every word, of the language from which we write, we become self-conscious, awkward and even blocked so that our voices are silenced. Writing from a woman's experience of life could mean that we reinscribe the roles with which we are familiar and perpetuate the structures of patriarchy. Or we could begin to notice the cracks, slip the trowel of language into those spaces and push, wiggle, and widen the gap, creating the "re-vision" of writing for women.

> just sit like I couldn't
> just sit down last night
> and write something

> So I think what you're saying
> about time is really
> an important thing.

Women writing? To be a writer, you must overcome resistance; you must want it enough to shove aside the room; to be a writer, you must be goal-driven and organized; to be a writer, you must give up all else. At least that is what some of the books about writing would have us believe. We need to offer time and devotion to the practice— all demands that ensure we will not likely be successful.

Yet, although we are metaphorically wringing our hands about time in the transcript, we still brought pieces to read, week after week. There was always writing from all of us. Somehow, we were finding time to write. I returned to the poem again to think about what might lie beneath our words.

So how can
I guess you learn to write
under those constraints.
I mean—look—
out of incredible horrible circumstances,
great literature is born
but my god.

Bringing our writing to a small group as we did, reading those pieces, talking about them and discussing the context of their creation raised issues and constraints that surrounded the work we were doing. By verbalizing those efforts and then revisiting the transcripts, we could question our assumptions, think through some of the effects on our writing, and make decisions about continuing, resisting or subverting. Through that process, we seemed more able to go away from the group and write. I never write as successfully as when I am in a group where we work with and speak of writing. Our relationship as writers helps us articulate the experience of being women writers and examine the challenges and possibilities more closely. We gain a toehold in the cracks.

Sometimes
there's little windows
like right now for me
where I can do it,

Re-text: Returning Another Time

The first time I read the transcript reflexively and then re-read it a number of times to write the original chapter, I thought the issue of time was about being women, about having the demands from partners, children, other people's children through our teaching, and the worth that society attributes to women's opinions. That presence is still there of course. The social construction of roles that women take on and that others expect of them are an issue. Yet my reading of this transcript feels broader and deeper this time.

Returning to the transcript after an absence of five years is an interesting opportunity for re-interpretation. I am less attached to the piece because the circumstances of its creation have mellowed with time; however, I recognized how the research, writing and thinking that I have done in the years hence have deepened my understanding of the challenges for women writing. I have a greater appreciation for the complexity of this issue and how it is not just a question of blaming these feelings on the position of women historically and culturally. Rather, this time I am much more willing to look at my own implication in constructing this role and understanding that it is not as simple as "writing from my experience." The patterns of a lifetime of language usage influence every moment of writing and bringing an ongoing reflexivity to such work is challenging at best.

What this rereading has offered me is the opportunity to understand how a small piece of text can continue being evocative and meaningful. For me, it is a measure of my shifting sense of subjectivity and my changing relationship to the practice of writing. This process reminds me that interpretation is not fixed, that we understand events in relation to our experience, and that such interpretive work shifts our connection to the past and the future that is unfolding. Moi explained that "Inscribing a specific context for a text does not *close* or *fix* the meaning of that text once and for all: there is always the possibility of reinscribing it within other contexts, a possibility that is indeed in principle boundless, and that is *structural* to any piece of language (1985, p. 155). We can explore those "infinite pasts."

Returning to this piece of transcript in another five years may be an interesting ritual to re-enact to see where my thinking and style have traveled in the time between. Juxtaposing my earlier interpretation to this one revealed how the rhythm of my language and some of my diction has changed. These shifts, I believe, are closely implicated in my ongoing thinking about language and writing. As I need to interpret my understandings differently, I search for other ways to articulate and represent those understandings.

This chapter explored the dynamic possibilities of language. Even though societal forces, such as political and cultural institutions, attempt to contain or determine meanings, language can resist and release us into possibility as it represents the conceptions of our experience. Recognizing some of these discursive influences enables us to call them into question and to find ways that we can subvert them through our texts. In chapter 4, I explore how texts offer further possibilities for disruption and change.

chapter four

the subjunctive cottage

A narrative isn't something you pull along like a toy train, a perpetually thrusting indicative. It's this little subjunctive cottage by the side of the road. All you have to do is open the door and walk in.

– *Carol Shields*

C armen sat across from me in my office as she opened her journal. "This writing has helped me make some decisions," she said. "Things that I have been struggling with for some time. Writing put my life out on the page for me to think about."

At the time I was working with her, Carmen was a 67-year-old woman who had been in a difficult marriage for many years. She had volunteered to be part of my women's writing group although she had written nothing substantial for 50 years because, as she explained, something about the process I described seemed interesting to her. When she learned that she would not have to be a skilled writer, that the work could be private if she chose, and that I was more interested in what the writing process contributed to her experience, she felt safe enough to join. Now, after several months of work, she sat with me prepared to read some excerpts about her husband as in the following:

> I arrived home at about 2 pm. George was trying to organize a trip to the doctor because he had broken glass in his big toe. I dropped him off, came home, rushed to put potatoes and pork chops in the oven then went back to pick him up, not knowing that someone from Homecare was coming to make his supper. We got home and then I had to get his antibiotics at Guardian Drugs even though I felt exhausted. Yesterday George wanted a new telephone answering machine, so I had gone to Sears to pick it up. Now he decided that the old

machine still worked, so he wanted me to take the new one back. While I was out, he asked me to pick up some Travel Aids at Superstore. When I came home, George had a note on the cupboard saying that I had better move everything of mine to Mary's since I was talking about staying there anyway.

Carmen pointed out that this entry really characterized much of their relationship, which began in the 1950s, with specific demands around her role as a housewife. She explained that when a large insurance company had interviewed her husband for a job, they also interviewed her. "They would not give him the job until they had interviewed 'the wife,'" she said. "They had to be sure that I would agree to do everything I could to help him be a good insurance agent. I had to promise that I would have breakfast ready by 7:30, lunch by 12:00, and supper at 6:30 so he could get right back out selling. I also had to promise to have a clean white shirt available for him every day and to press his suit every night." The dynamics of such a structure continued right through their married life until, as she mentioned in her journal, he challenged her to leave him.

When I next saw Carmen, she had followed through on leaving, moving her belongings into Mary's house. She told me that her husband had phoned her one morning and threatened to commit suicide because her leaving had upset him so badly. "He hung up the phone before I could answer," Carmen said. "I didn't know what to do and fell into the guilt trap he set." She gave me her journal entry that chronicled her efforts to get outside help and not go back home, which she realized is what he wanted her to do. At the end of the ordeal, she wrote:

I am desperate to make George understand how unhappy I am and have been for 25–30 years. I've been unhappy about the way he treated and yelled at the kids. I've been unhappy about his control over all of us. I've asked him to treat us like he treats the neighbors—he's good to them.... Even if he committed suicide, it would be his choice—not mine. I am not responsible for his actions. I have covered for him and made excuses for him for so many years that I will have to keep telling myself—'it's not my fault.'

Although Carmen's story was difficult to read and to listen to, it also was a story of hope as every page she became clearer about how she was deciding to leave and what might lie ahead. In one of the last entries, she noted: "I get so depressed at times and feel really beaten. Upon looking back, I think these feelings are becoming less of a burden. I like to be in control of my life and rarely have been."

As her writing became a way of sorting out the conflicting voices and feelings that inundated her daily, Carmen moved from remembering the past and how she had been an independent young woman to remembering her transition into being a dependent wife. In the end, the writing became part of her decision to move away from her husband and begin a different life for herself.

In her examination of the healing effects of writing, Louise DeSalvo (1999) described how Virginia Woolf believed that moments of profound insight come from writing about a thoughtful examination of psychic wounds. Such a process makes us aware of ourselves, our relationship to others and our place in the world and helps to heal our sense of fracture and disconnection. The process of putting one's strong emotional experiences into writing gives voice to fears, dreams and disappointments. Through writing, we can see the experience more holistically, reflect on it, and connect it to other experiences in our lives and those around us. With the story in such a context, we can interpret the events and see how this piece fits with the greater pattern of our lives, often seeing directions we have taken and choosing new pathways or alternative routes.

In this chapter, I examine some of these structures of writing and their influence and effect on our work as writers. While narrative is a powerful way to tell stories and offer alternatives, creating what I call a "subjunctive space," other structures also offer productive opportunities for women.

The Work of Narrative and Beyond[1]

When we speak of telling stories, generally we understand those to be narratives that rely on the interest in disruption or surprise against the backdrop of the habitual rhythm of our daily life. "Every day, I drive the same way to work," we might say to a friend, "but you'll never guess what happened today." And so the story begins. What has changed our usual expectations? We build detail upon detail, leading up to a climax or punch line or significant moment. Jerome Bruner (1990) has suggested that it is through the telling of such narratives that we construct a version of ourselves in the world. Narratives arrange events, summon characters, and create metaphors and other tropes that weave a cultural fabric that not only brings meaning to our actions but also creates a milieu in which we can act. Our subjectivity unfolds within the pages of our stories. Gertrude Stein, in writing about identity, said that it was "not a thing that exists but something you do or do not remember" (cited in Elliot & Wallace, 1995, p. 164). Narratives are a way of remembering that also give shape to that process.

We thread the moments of our lives with other experiences to develop a sense of wholeness, albeit a whole that is changed and extended. We explain that we did not get the new job because it was not meant to be and that something better will be coming along. We imagine dramatic scenarios before we break up with a lover and then we "rewrite" the event afterwards, an event that can go through many versions depending on whom we tell and what our memories are. The process is one of "emplotment" (Kerby, 1991) where one causally connects discrete events into a narrative structure that generates an understanding of her or his past. Carmen's narration of her life with George helped her to understand the difficult relationship and her need to change those circumstances. For her, the kind of wife and mother she had believed herself to be, the size of house she lived in, the number of belongings she owned, and her relationship to her community were all changing. Writing was a way of interpreting this life she was leaving but also of beginning to understand the shape of the emerging one.

In all the groups, women wrote many pieces about their lives, but there was not a particular structure to those stories. Rather than always following traditional narrative patterns, the writing often deviated from those forms through poetry, journal entries, or snippets that ranted, rejoiced or mourned. Sometimes the writers drew pictures and created collages. At times, the women wrote in first person with intimate voices while at other times, they chose a third-person perspective and relied on greater fictionalizing. The responses were fragmented and multileveled, revealing lives that were not being neatly explained by coherent narratives. The collection of writing resembled an abstract painting rather than a realistic scene; it was a complex picture of varied lives filled with pleasure and difficulty. I recognized that writing was not creating a plotted, consistent story of the "self" for these women, but that understanding their lives through writing demanded a different kind of structure—something that reflected the fragmentary nature of their experience.

Carol Shields described a similar experience in her writing that found her searching for a way to move from the traditional narrative to find a structure that more closely related to the shape of her experience:

A story had to have conflict, it was said. A story consisted of a problem and a solution; I believed that too. A story must contain the kind of characters that the reader can relate to; well, yes, of course. Every detail provided in a short story must contribute to its total effect; well, if Chekhov and Hemingway said so, then it had to be true. The structure of a story could be diagrammed on a blackboard, a gently inclined line representing the rising action, then a sudden escalatory peak, followed by a steep plunge which demonstrated the denouement and then the resolution. I remember feeling quite worshipful in the presence of that ascending line. Very tidy, very tight, the short story as boxed kit, as scientific demonstration, and furthermore it was teachable. (1993, p. 244)

Not until Shields found herself caught and frustrated in the middle of writing a novel did she consider different ways of structuring narrative. She decided to shelve her novel and to experiment with possibilities, writing in whatever direction the work seemed to take her. She described the resulting year as one of the most pleasurable of her writing career. There was a reckless happiness to her work and a sense that she owned what she was writing: "every word, every comma. The small chilly bedroom where I had my desk in those days felt crowded with noisy images. Strange images. Subversive images" (p. 245).

Some of her stories did not have conflicts and strong, central characters, or they had a disturbing mix of realism and fantasy. One short story, "Home," is about the invisible threads of coincidence that link individuals to others in the world where one is left with a deep satisfaction and sense of hope in having read it. This was the power, Shields noted, of the material shaping her stories rather than the theory. She also paid attention to the pattern of women's oral stories and thought about how such designs could influence her narratives. She observed that women tended to sit together and recount episodic events with digressions and little side stories rather than telling linear tales and that they often would throw "their narrative scraps into a kind of kitty and make them a larger story" (p. 249).

In her writing, she wanted to embrace such contradictions, the tentativeness, the episodic, and the jumble of memories. To her such writing was more realistic than "the spine of a traditional story, that holy line of rising action that is supposed to lead somewhere important, somewhere inevitable, modeled perhaps on the orgasmic pattern of tumescence followed by detumescence, an endless predictable circle of desire, fulfillment, and quiescence" (p. 248). The appeal of a more random or disorderly narrative for Shields was that it offered a semblance of the texture of women's ordinary lives rather than a recounting of personal battles to be won and goals to be obtained.

Toni Morrison, in recognizing the possibilities in writing, suggested, "narrative is not and never has been enough, just as the object drawn on a canvas or a cave wall is never simply mimetic" (1984, p. 388). Morrison described the potential in writing between, through, and beyond narrative. To acknowledge such openness means one recognizes writing to be more complex and less easily defined and categorized. Gail Scott wrote:

> we keep writing the (poetic) story, the (poetic) novel – further imbued with a little theory: i.e., commentary signifying that place where our writing processes consciously meet the politics of the women's community (as well as contemporary strategies for writing).... Now, I think, for me at any rate, it's precisely where the poetic and the personal enter the essay form that thought steps over its former boundaries. (1989, p. 106)

In chapter 1, I noted how Friedman (1994), within the context of social constructionism, echoed similar thinking about narrative structure and identified four ways in which women's writing has deconstructed and reconstructed narrative: using existing structures to write their own ideologies, reconfiguring narrative patterns, weaving oral and narrative conventions, and creating a collaborative dialogue in their work between forms.

Friedman described the more open boundary between the poetic and narrative in her discussion of women poets. She noted how the right and necessity for poets to claim historical and mythic discourse "permeates the interplay of lyric and narrative in women's contemporary long poems" (1994, p. 38). Within such poetry, she explained, women use direct narrative to tell a story or arrange lyrical sequences that the reader can (re)construct as an implicit story. Narrative also can exist on the borderline of such poems, connecting a series of shorter, lyrical pieces together. In these long poems, Friedman suggested, narrative and lyric "coexist in a collaborative interchange of different and independent discourses" (p. 23).

By way of illustration, Friedman refers to the work of poet-historian Irena Klepfisz. Klepfisz's long poem, *Keeper of Accounts,* is in four parts and deals with the poet's survival in a post-Holocaust world. "The textual practices of the poem," Friedman wrote, "construct a subject very much in process and on trial—caught in the processes of retrieving forgotten histories of a childhood in Poland, on trial as a Jew who survived the Holocaust by 'passing' as a Polish child, who must now reclaim her Jewish legacy and identity" (p. 33). The long poem has different discourses juxtaposed throughout. For instance, one section, "Work Sonnets with Notes and a Monologue," consists of three parts: a verse, notes, and a prose monologue. Throughout, Klepfisz established a dialogue between the symbolic and semiotic where the gaps both act as grammatical pauses and as spaces that resist language and reveal the hesitation of the unspeakable pain and yearning of the Holocaust (p. 38).

The blurring of genre boundaries is not what is crucial for women's writing, however. Rather it is the possibility of choices in writing the text that most clearly reflects the experiences about which they write whether they combine the fictional and poetic techniques in an essay such as Scott's "Spaces Like Stairs" (1989) (an excerpt of which appears in the first chapter) or call on the lyric to create a poem like Di Brandt's "the one who lives underwater" (1987). Sometimes, being able to move beyond the narrative and the prosaic is the only way of writing, as Brandt explained:

> I couldn't write prose because I kept getting stuck in the sentences: once you started you had to say whatever the syntax prescribed. I wanted every sentence to have the whole world in it, concentric circles of world, waves and curls of it. With poetry it was the opposite: the lines crumbled fell away, short, broken, twisted, without breath, because of the fear of God (and my father's hand) in it. (1996, p. 14)

Sometimes, too, because poetry attends to the spaces around the words and between the words and margins, such writing is the only way women can come to understand their own silencing and silences. "Each poem has its own silence," M. Nourbese Philip (1994, p. 295) wrote. A silence that shapes the text as much as the words and helps to define the poem: a silence that has its own grammar, its own language.

In the writing groups, we challenged each other to explore different kinds of writing. Rather than trying to tell our stories like coherent narratives, we created writing practices that offered more fragmented glimpses and opened up spaces for possibility. Texts, prompts, objects, and pictures became sources for bits of writing. As our collection of "bits" grew, so did our conversations about what those pieces pointed to and what they might mean.

While the work was fragmented, there was a meaningful presence to it. From the uncertain and the partial, we were recognizing a pattern of writing that described women's experience. I could understand this productive scene by thinking about Hayles' comparison between the deconstruction of texts and chaos theory: both are uncertain, fragmented but also fecund.

I continued to wonder, however, if it was not necessary for us to create narratives to understand our experience, how did writing illuminate the possibilities of our lives?

Writing and the Subjunctive Space

The writer experiences a tension between her desire to illustrate the entirety of an experience and an awareness that moments of such coherence are illusory, never able to achieve the fullness she imagines. In writing, she knows that she has not reached the ideal expression and is left desiring a way to say more, or say it more clearly, or to find just the right combination of words. What writers long to describe seems always just before them.

Kristeva (1980) described the importance of demystifying this desire for language to be universal and unifying. If language were so encompassing, interpretation would stop, leaving our lives stagnate and rigid. Instead, in a biological existence that is ever emerging and changing, our symbolic realm also must allow for the multiplicity of an individual's identifications just as Grosz spoke about a multiplicity of pasts. As Kristeva pointed out, language is an open structure that one can transgress and which continually produces change and renewal through discursive practices; thus writers like Shields are able to transgress more traditional structures of language and describe the fluid nature of their experience.

This very inability to create an encompassing wholeness in our written texts is what invites others to our writing. The openness of such texts and the gaps in meaning offer a space where our readers can engage with that experience. The gaps in the text create what Iser (1978) called an "element of indeterminacy" that initiates a performance of meaning rather than formulating meaning itself. Bruner (1986) suggested that such a text subjunctivizes reality; that is, it denotes an action or state as conceived rather than as fact, used to express a contingent, hypothetical or prospective event. The subjunctive reveals human possibilities rather than settled certainties.

Bruner uses the term "subjunctive reality" primarily in regard to narrative; however, remembering Friedman's explanation of the four ways women both use and move beyond narrative, I suggest subjunctive reality is important for most writing in the literary realm—fiction, poetry, autobiography, and memoir, for example. Writing, then, becomes a site of possibility, a place of "as if" that works in multiple ways with, through, and beyond the text. For the writer and for the reader, they write and read *as if* the text can describe the reality of an event, an imagining, or a feeling; *as if* language did not remove us a step from it. Such contingencies broaden the possibilities for experiencing, acting, understanding, and creating.

The writing in the women's group included a range of genres and reflected their actual experiences in varying degrees. Of course, trying to identify which elements in a person's writing have actually happened to her and which have not is a futile exercise. Rather, when I suggest that the writing reflected their experience, I am describing how the women thought about their pieces and how deeply implicated they saw their lives in the work. For instance, one woman considered the events in her life quite carefully as she explored some incidents from her childhood through memoir. Another chose to use only a few elements of her experience as a high school teacher to write a novel about the Virgin Mary, giving the character a 1990s flavor by using the slang of the high school girls she taught and depending on Biblical and other historical research for most of the details.

The women also saw some of their work as less imagined than other pieces, but even for those where the writers claimed they were writing exactly as it had happened, they still had to re-imagine the events before writing and in doing so, chose some details and omitted others as well as reorganizing them to suit a particular audience. When asked, Sophia, who had been adamant that she was writing about an event just as it had occurred, admitted that she had made up some details to make the story more believable and interesting. When someone suggested that her story showed good imagination, however, Sophia still insisted that she had not imagined anything; it was entirely true.

As Sophia's response suggests, "imaginative" often is a qualifying term used to evaluate writing. Saying that someone's work is imaginative means that the writer offers an unusual or interesting perspective on what we might call the everyday or ordinary. Most of the women in the writing groups, though, would shy away from such a term, suggesting that their work is not that good or, like Sophia, they would not see a role for imagination in a "real" event.

Nevertheless, imagining is connected to our lived experience even while it moves us beyond the "real world" to reconfigure contexts and events of experience. Kendall Walton (1990) described a form of imagining he calls *de se* where people imagine themselves doing, watching or experiencing something, or being in a certain way as opposed to just imagining that something happens to oneself. For example, I may imagine that someone will offer me an exciting job and envisage the tasks I might perform and the pay I might receive—such is *de se* imagining. If I simply dream that someone will offer me an unspecified job, the engagement with such imagining is less detailed and specific and differs from the former experience. From our *de se* imaginings, fictional truths and a fictional world arise.

Walton defined fictional truths as a specific call in a particular context to imagine something. One can think of the game of playing house as an example based on Walton's understanding of fictional truths. The fictional proposition is that one is to imagine playing house in order to participate in the game. While it is true that one is playing house, the proposition that one is living in and keeping a house is fictional. The fact that it is fictional is a fictional truth.

The difference between the imagined and the fictional is implicit in Walton's definition in that a sense of agreement is present in the fictional but not necessarily in the imagined. Mary Rogers (1991) described this social sense of the fictive as implicit agreements to act *as if* some things are "true, obvious, or at least plausible enough not to necessitate questioning." She adds that the fictive is "a deeply but silently social 'Let's pretend'" (p. 208).

This sense of the "as if" can be related to writers and their ability to subjunctivize reality. The propositions of what was to be imagined were laid out by the women writers: we were to imagine that a story was true in the real world (Sophia's) or we were to imagine it true in a fictional world (Virgin Mary story). In any case, such fictional truths created fictional worlds where possibilities became more evident and where the writers could respond *as if* things were true in the real world, the distinction between the real world and fictional ones being in the manner in which they are made.

> A particular work of fiction, in its context, establishes its fictional world and generates the fictional truths belonging to it. A particular biography or history does not itself establish the truth of what it says or produce the facts it is concerned with. What generates facts, if they are our own creations, is not individual pieces of writing but something more like the whole body of a culture's discourse or the language itself as opposed to what is said in the language, or the conceptual scheme embodied in either of these. (Walton, p. 102)

There is the sense of communal agreement, the social "we" that establishes the fictive. We agree to act "as if" something exists. In talking about the book *Tom Sawyer*, one might say that "Tom Sawyer was lost in a cave" rather than "In the story, Tom Sawyer was lost in the cave" because in speaking of fiction, we speak as if we were referring to a real person who existed.

The subjunctive power of a text, therefore, lies partly in our collective agreement to imagine, to agree as if that world existed. In conjunction with our social and cultural understandings are features of texts that further invite the reader to enter the subjunctive cottage. Bruner suggested three particular discourse features that create such a possibility. First is the use of presupposition, which Bruner defined as an "implied proposition whose force remains invariant whether the explicit proposition in which it is embedded is true or false" (1986, p. 27). For instance in saying that John did or did not see a chimera establishes the presupposition that there is a chimera and provides a way to mean more than what is said. This feature can be related to Walton's notion of the fictional truth. The second discourse feature is subjectification, or the filter of the protagonist's consciousness from which the story emerges. Through such a perspective, one can understand the reality of the events from the characters' points of view by becoming privy to other minds. A third feature Bruner suggested is the use of multiple perspectives that view the world "simultaneously through a set of prisms each of which catches some part of it" (p. 26) such as when one particular event is told from different viewpoints.

Gary Morson offered another perspective of the subjunctive (1994). Drawing from the work of Bahktin, he described how different genres define a field of possibilities; that is, there is a particular time and space available in which events can occur—what Bahktin called "a chronotope." This variety of story shapes offers multiple world views and a realm of possible events. "In such a world, time ramifies and its possibilities multiply; each realized possibility opens new choices while precluding others that once could have been made" (p. 22).

Within a text, Morson pointed out, there are the choices taken and those passed over; yet even those unactualized possibilities can leave their mark on history. A present, therefore, can grow partly from an unrealized past. The traces of paths taken and untaken in a text, Morson calls "sideshadowing" which "leads to the subjunctive and the contrary-to-fact conditional: what if, if only had it not been, were it not for—what would have taken place then? . . . Sideshadowing restores *the possibility of possibility*. Its most fundamental lesson is: to understand a moment is to grasp not only what did happen but also what might have happened" (pp. 118–119).

Morson goes on to delineate the character of sideshadowing by drawing from the novels of Dostoevsky, which have some of the more complex manifestations of the effects of choices made and not made. While Morson points out how an accomplished author represents the richness of choice through the characters in his novel, making choices is also part of the process of writing and even those without the skill of Dostoevsky create texts that are landscapes of directions taken and the shadows of those left behind.

Nancy Welch (1998) used the concept of sideshadowing to develop a revision process with student writers. She suggested students and teachers examine possible directions and other choices for the text at each moment. Students reflected on their texts in the margins and the teacher engaged in dialogue with the student's exploration of possibility.

I have used a similar focus with writers by interviewing them about their texts asking about their decisions, directions they have taken, the wonderings they have about choices not made, and their questions about what their writing reveals. For instance, I interviewed one young woman who wrote a short descriptive narrative set in a busy train station. The one-page piece was about the moment of breaking up with a boyfriend. I followed her description of the event with busy images of the train station and the contrasting thoughts of the woman as she prepares to tell her companion that their relationship is over. The scene she has written feels quite innocuous until the line: "Before she could move in for the kill, she would have to ready herself." This shift in tone and metaphor was one that I marked. When I asked her about the line, she said that it had been unconscious. "It's the rewriting that counts more than the original stream-of-consciousness," she said. But as we spoke further about her piece, I could see that she was somewhat shaken by her choice of words and that she was beginning to see the writing in a way she had not before. In our discussion, those words seemed to be a glimpse of the anger that women are discouraged from expressing and she seemed to be seeing some of the power behind her feelings.

Such conversations have the potential to open up the text, both past and future, and help clarify the author's current choices. Through this collaborative work, the writer often is able to determine the center of gravity that brings a coherent pattern to her or his text and to make decisions about what information to elaborate and what to eliminate as well as gain some insight about her understanding of a particular experience.

Texts are sites of contingency and possibility. In a way that lived experience does not allow, through writing we can imagine the fullness of time and the patterns of choice. Within the subjunctive spaces of writing, one can realize the complexity of experience while the very openness of writing and the consideration of possibilities call into question what we have assumed.

For the women, exploring the shape of possibilities was "forming living" and in so doing, they acknowledged some of the limits to their sense of self. Opening up the subjunctive spaces of writing also increased their sense of risk. This effect was never clearer than in Carmen's experience. She had finally, after months of worry about her abilities, established a ritual of writing every evening, but then another worry appeared. "When I wrote down how angry I was at my husband," she said, "then it suddenly seemed true. I wondered if he might find this." She discovered hiding places for her journals and during one of our interviews, I agreed to receive and destroy her journals should anything happen to her. "Writing is different than thinking these feelings to yourself," she said. "But I'm glad to be doing it now. I think I cheated myself out of memories by not doing it before."

Writing is a risky business, our thinking shaped on the page for others to ponder, consider, judge. There seems to be so much of our experience, our imagination reshaped in the text and existing in a space of its own. Writers struggle with both the desire and resistance they feel toward writing especially women who are writing in ways that question patriarchy. They struggle to overcome their reluctance to challenge conventional structures. Then, when they find the courage to write and perhaps subvert canonized practices, there may be resistance and strong reactions from others who do not want to hear what they are suggesting. Nevertheless, through writing, through creating a subjunctive space, writers can see meaningful patterns in their lives and explore the potentials of certain paths.

When I interviewed Carmen again at the end of the group, I asked her what role the writing had had in her decision to leave her husband. The writing, she told me, had not caused her to leave but had helped her see the unfolding of her life as it had been and as it could be. The work in her journals had helped her begin to imagine life without her husband and to make some choices about how that would happen.

The Complexity of the Subjunctive

Complexity theorists' study of living systems has shown that such structures are self-organizing. That is, as a nonlinear network of patterns, they operate far from equilibrium and create new structures and modes of behavior.

Humberto Maturana, in his study of the nervous system, suggested that such a system was not only self-organizing but also self-referring. Living systems were, in Maturana's view, cognitive systems and living itself was a process of cognition. In his work with Francisco Varela, he described this circular organization as autopoiesis. As Capra explains: "*Auto*, of course, means 'self' and refers to the autonomy of self-organizing systems; and *poiesis*—which shares the same Greek root as the word 'poetry'—means 'making.' So *autopoiesis* means 'self-making'" (1996, p. 97). A feature of such patterns is self-reinforcing feedback. A change, even a small one, in one area of the network propagates through the entire system, modifying its character.

Drawing on complexity theory, Finke has pointed out how these ideas are isomorphic to the work of literature:

[Using] a more complex, 'disorderly' model, societies both maintain themselves and change through elaborate feedback mechanisms by which their cultural productions—individuals, genders, class identities, and written texts—feed back into them, reorganizing and reproducing social structures and the strategies that maintain and refashion them. (1992, p. 9)

Writing and writers, as part of this larger network of cultural productions, are influenced by the energies of such contexts; however, on a smaller scale, within the work of one writer writing one piece of text, similar feedback processes are at work. In writing, just by describing an experience, I perceive that event differently and may suggest other directions, other paths—the potentials of the sideshadow. Writing about that moment has changed it.

For the women, by writing about aspects of their lives, they reinterpreted those events and in doing so could see other choices they might make, other endings to the story, new paths to take. Carmen's choices were perhaps the most dramatic, but all the women experienced the power of writing in making them aware of the possibilities—and sometimes the very real difficulty of those possibilities—that were open to them.

Opening Texts

The young women met for some time as a writing group before they began to risk exploring possibilities in a text. The greatest feat at first was just reading their writing to the group. Those early pieces focused on familiar topics, mostly narratives of love. Genevieve brought a poem to the group a section of which follows:

I remember a couple of months ago
I met him
We sat at a little table all night
In a restaurant across town
It was New Year's

And I was still getting over my
first boyfriend
He seemed so nice
I liked him for a long time after that
And he was only 17
For sure he couldn't pull the
"But you're so YOUNG!"
No
He pulled the
"But I'm friends with your sister!
How could I go out with you?
Besides …
I'm in grade 12."
In other words
Basically the same thing
I just smile and laugh
You can bet that hurts …

Di Brandt (1996) described how, in her experience as a visiting writer in schools, the girls she worked with primarily wrote about love and their great anxiety around that subject. "It's a particular kind of love," she wrote. "It's highly conventionalized, abstracted, full of wispy clouds and unicorns and fluffy kittens and fluttering hearts and, running through everything, a deep sense of loss, grief over the beloved's absence" (p. 15). Such a response is not surprising, Brandt pointed out, because the students have spent a number of years in school learning how to think abstractly and learning how not to attend to the body. In my work with young writers, I realized, too, how hard it was for them to actually express concrete experiences that engaged the body. They responded as if it were a bit strange and perhaps even embarrassing.

Their abstract romantic pieces were laden with sadness. When I asked them why they did not follow the typical romance structure of happy endings, Genevieve suggested that she found it superficial to write happy endings because it seemed fake to her. "Life's not really like that," she said. "Everything doesn't end in happy endings.

So most everything I write is sad." The other girls agreed. They saw their writing as a protest, a rendering of the dream that patriarchy had handed them colored by the recognition that it was all imaginary, that no one could love them as totally and perfectly as promised. So why did they write these stories at all? Brandt suggested that

> These young women, on the cusp of adulthood, didn't want to acknowledge the betrayal of the world, of boyfriend and fathers, and of men in general, so they wouldn't have to acknowledge self-hatred, deep down, so they wouldn't feel worthless, abandoned, discriminated against, threatened, because they were women. (p. 16)

Even though the girls had experienced disappointment and disillusionment, they could not completely give up the dream whose discursive structures had shaped so much of their understanding of being female. And without access to other discourses, what would they write about? One of the more powerful effects of a writing group for young women, we believed, was the opportunity to offer different ways of speaking and writing. If such opportunities are not specifically pointed to, girls, who are inundated by narrowly defined ultra-feminine images in the media and through popular culture, may not realize them.

Janice Radway (1983), in her study of women who read romances, suggested that women return again and again to that genre as a way of satisfying needs created by a patriarchal culture that is unable, at the same time, to fulfill those needs. With the girl's writing, they saw the romance as a story available to them and as one that would not be neatly resolved. In their stories, even as they searched for unity and happiness, they undermined its possibility and the reality of it happening. As Sophia explained to me, "We don't write happy endings because it doesn't happen that way in real life. The way I see it is that people who are writing romances are writing for the moment because a lot of women will get sucked in and they're just giving them the fantasy all the time. They want to be happy, but to try to sit down and write something like that with a happy ending? No way."

Within the girls' romance writing, however, lay the possibility for calling into question some of the societal roles assigned to women. Although they did not necessarily see their writing as undermining the romantic story of patriarchy, their choice of how to tell such stories suggested that further imaginative writing might open up different possibilities for them to consider.

Poet Ted Hughes (1967) wrote that "All imaginative writing is to some extent the voice of what is neglected or forbidden, hence its connection with a past in a nostalgic vein and the future in a revolutionary vein" (p. 51). I wondered if by challenging the girls to go further in their imaginative writing, they might move beyond the romance story and write pieces that had some revolutionary possibility for their future rather than the sense of entrapment their romance stories held.

After meeting as a group for some months, the girls expressed a desire to push their writing beyond the comfortable level it had reached at which time we introduced the Jeanette Winterson piece described earlier, inviting them to write "the forbidden." They returned to the group somewhat amazed by what they had accomplished and felt ready to give public voice to their words.

The language that constrained them, influenced their lives in profound ways echoed in these excerpts from a cafe reading they chose to do for their parents and friends:

Be polite, curtsy well, love men your own age,
never fight or swear, respect your elders. You
are a girl. Nothing more.

> *the forbidden worms into the heart and mind until what one*
> *truly desires*
> *had been encased in the dark walls of what one ought to*
> *desire*
> *to hear clearly the voices that have whispered at her*
> *for so many years.*

You dominate my dreams
But everything is not as it seems

> *The world around her forbids her*
> *to write, to express. It is considered*
> *childish and considered reaching for*
> *something that is not there. So they are*
> *saying that she is denied the freedom*
> *to imagine and express ... She refuses to*
> *live like this and stands up*
> *against all the*
> *criticism and discrimination.*
> *There are no limits for her,*
> *no rules, and if any,*
> *she breaks them all.*

As she sits in her tree, she remembers the Barbie doll that she had so long ago. She thought of how nice Barbie would have looked in jeans, a T-shirt, and with no hair. She decides that perfection must be altered even if it is forbidden.

Writing offered an opportunity to use language differently. For the girls, this meant writing beyond just the sad ending to express their anger and frustration at the heterosexual romance as constructed in our society.

The theme of "forbidden writing" continued to play out in the group and the girls were eager to press further into exploration of their texts. We turned to the work of German feminist and sociologist Frigga Haug (1987) for some direction. Haug, as part of a group of women, met over a period of several years to write about the sexualization of females. The group wrote about their memories of body/sexual experiences (for example, breasts or legs) in the third person that they then read aloud to the others.

The aspect of the study that seemed most useful for us was the discourse analysis that was part of the women's search for understanding.[2] Using a similar approach to analysing text, we divided the girls' writing into categories of wishes or dreams, actions, and feelings. Breaking apart the text and seeing the words in clusters stopped the usual response to the writing and allowed the writer and readers to see more clearly the historical, cultural, and social traces in the writing.

For the next round of "forbidden writing," we agreed to write in third person and when the pieces were read aloud, I realized that the effect of this point of view created a small sense of distance from the text that would make the next step—the breaking apart of the text into wishes, actions, and feelings—easier. Alexis's piece about her incident with the neighbour boy that I referred to in chapter 3 was an example from that writing that I want to return to in more detail here as an example of this process. Alexis wrote:

> He laid his navy blue kangaroo jacket neatly on the ground and was sitting next to it. With a look of anticipation on his face, he gave the ground an inviting pat. It was a grandpa wants you to sit on his knee pat. He is nice, she thought, he put his jacket down for me so I would not get dirty ... She looks back now and realizes he was probably covering his own ass. He tried to unzip her pants, but his hands were shaky and the zipper got stuck. He tugged at it fiercely; finally he just slid his hands into her panties and touched her in her private place. It went on for less than a minute ....

After reading this piece, I helped Alexis sort through the actions, feelings, dreams and wishes emerging from the text, creating three lists. As we did so, the girls noticed an interesting trend. Sophia said, "When you read it, it sounded like it was from a child. Reading it here, it sounds more traumatic." They noticed the violent words juxtaposed with words of reconciliation: playing guns, stung, caught, warning, keep quiet, stop, throw, tear, screaming, crying, cursing, struggle. Then: understands, kisses, whispers. And the feelings: freedom, worry, terrifying, healing, dumb, silly, sad, anger.

It was at this point that Alexis expressed the ambivalence she still felt about the event and referred to the final lines where she connects the narrative to a current boyfriend.

What became clear in working with the girls through this kind of analysis was the complexity and contradictions of their experiences. In some ways, our group added another layer of complexity to their lives by focusing their attention on feminist discourses that had been previously fragmented phrases and opinions for them. The meetings became a time for girls to make comments and declarations (feminist in character) that they might not make so vociferously in other places such as their comments about body weight and Barbie dolls.

At the same time, the group was a place to explore real or desired heterosexual relationships where some of the girls teetered between declaring their independence and self-determination and collapsing other hopes into the attentions of a young man. The discourse of the group, developed within this context of a feminist perspective, also became a location to highlight the contradictory nature of women's lives. Even as we talked about how the media, our culture, our stories influenced and shaped us, we could not stop the siren calls that moved us to longing.

Wendy Hollway (1989) suggested that within competing and contradictory discourses, one will take a position in a certain discourse rather than another because there is an investment or *cathexis*, in other words, there is some possibility of satisfaction or a payoff even if that is not fulfilled. I wondered, sometimes, how often the girls chose to take a position in the feminist or heterosexual discourse just for the comfort level of the group. In any case, I realized the difficulty of reshaping language with "our own intentions," as Bakhtin described, when it is often so hard for young women to even know what those intentions are. In comparison, Carmen had taken forty years to begin to sort out her intentions and to feel some control in her life.

Yet, Carmen's experience reveals how the interactions between circumstances and her writing helped clarify those intentions and led her to action. The same possibilities were evident for the girls. Through the work of the group, we had begun to raise an awareness of their language, the *as if* potential, that they were beginning to shape with their own intentions as a way into action and creation of a story of their own. The clearest indication of this occurred when the girls planned the public reading described above and when Alexis and Pegatha developed the play with the scene about lesbian relationships.

For the writers, the spaces created by the group became one way of finding the encouragement and courage to continue questioning and exploring their lives through writing. The groups became places where talk about writing explored relations and possibilities for living that they might have judged too dangerous in more public places. We spoke as if some things were true or as if we could lead our lives in particular ways. We told stories about ourselves and others: some were actual experiences; some were unfulfilled wishes or fantasies. *What would happen if?* Because the writing was not confined to one form, the range of options in style and responses further developed the sense of possibility.

Although some welcome changes occurred through the writing, the possibilities that emerged were not always positive. Sometimes realizations were difficult and sometimes there was little correspondence between the writing and understanding. For example, although the girls wrote severe indictments against Barbie and her symbolic function as the "perfect female," many of them still worried obsessively about their weight and body size. At times, the writing seemed to further complicate already complex lives.

Rita Felski (1989) suggested that if women consider the political function of art, their work can disrupt the structures of symbolic discourse through which patriarchal culture is constituted. The experimental and innovative text, the avant-garde, is one way to disrupt the conventional, the expected, the unquestioned. While Felski pointed out that "fragmentation and subversion of patterns do not in themselves bear any relationship to a feminist position" and will not do so unless it undermines a patriarchal ideological position (p. 32), I suggest that interrupting the familiar structures through which this discourse is constituted will support a move to writing otherwise— a move that takes us beyond the undermining into shaping different futures. Through writing in the future perfect, Irigaray created the possibility of "woman" in the symbolic order. What women have to say as well as how they say it is important.

Gail Scott (1989), in wondering how women actually choose a form in which to write, speculated that there was a connection between the form women choose and the circumstances of their lives. The forms in the groups ranged from journal entries to poetry to short fiction, with the sentence structure, gaps and pauses creating an emotional character for the work. Once the writers knew they did not have to follow particular structures or expectations, they chose a variety of texts and often wrote fragments as representations of their experience.

The importance of form seemed most clear with the girls' writing when we broke their texts in categories rather than leaving it in prosaic or poetic form such as the example with Alexis's story described earlier. The listing of words from her story broke apart the syntax, stopped the rhythm and clarified some of the emotion behind the writing. In one sense, it felt as if we had filtered out what might be called the semiotic chora (Kristeva, 1980), so the words, in this new context, seemed different somehow but still with traces of their former intentions. Some of those intentions seemed surprising when revealed in such a way.

At the same time, clearing some of the influences of the semiotic chora from their language, reinforced how much more is revealed through the writing than just the language that is chosen. The rhythms that are created from particular words being in prox-imity to each other, the silences, the line breaks, and the punctuation create sensations that are difficult to describe in language but that can be clearly felt when the words are read. Not only do our words reveal some of our intentions, aspirations, designs, or aims, but also how we choose to say them.

Writing is a site of possibility where we can learn things about ourselves, where we imagine different choices, and where we reconfigure our experience. We create conditions to become other than what we are or have been. My work, my "story," as a writer and a teacher depends on this kind of imaginative possibility, the vision of the *as if.* These rich, *as if* hypothetical worlds (our own or those of others' creations) change our experiences to make them less fa-miliar so that we can become conscious of "what is not yet, of what might, unpredictably, still be experienced" (Greene, 1995, p. 92).

When I teach writing or work with writers in classrooms or elsewhere, I focus on offering such opportunities to see and imagine possibilities. I think it is important to increase awareness toward language with its power to shape us even as we shape and use it. Then, as writers, we can choose options that may be different from what is expected or sanctioned and make decisions with more awareness, enriching our sense of subjectivity and our power to act in the world.

How we realize some of those possibilities in writing is facilitated through the participation with others. Rereading the transcripts of the meetings revealed how often the conversations helped interpretations evolve and how writers had the opportunity to articulate their intentions and be more conscious of the processes of writing.

The importance of the group was borne out by Carmen. As I described in chapter 1, the group structure with the older women did not transpire as I had hoped and I ended up with individual meetings where we discussed their writing. After her participation in my research, Carmen joined a women's writing group for an eight-week session, exploring spirituality through writing. Although she felt more discomfort at times with having to be part of a larger collective, her thinking and writing developed quickly and her insights deepened through such interaction. In my work as a writer and researcher, I continue to understand groups as rich interpretive structures for writing, which is the focus for the next chapter.

Notes

1. This section and the following one originally appeared in a slightly different version in my article "As If Women Writing," published in *Journal of Literacy Research,* 1999.
2. Brigitte Hipfl from the University of Klagenfurt explained this aspect of Haug's work to me. She had been involved in a research project with Haug where this kind of discourse analysis was used.

chapter five

in the company of writers

You are the company you keep ...

— *Gregory Bateson*

In 1927, Canadian artist, Emily Carr, received an invitation from Eric Brown of the National Gallery in Ottawa to send some of her work for an exhibition and to come east herself for the opening. He also suggested that she stop in Toronto to meet some landscape painters called the Group of Seven—a meeting that proved to be propitious for Emily because she saw in their canvases the kind of intensity that she had be struggling to represent. "I'm way behind them in drawing and in composition and rhythm and planes," she wrote, "but I know inside me what they're after and I feel that perhaps, given a chance, I could get it too. Ah, how I have wasted the years! But there are still a few left" (1966, p. 6). Later, she expressed more fully the impact their work and insights had had on her:

> Oh, God, what have I seen? Where have I been? ... Chords way down in my being have been touched ... Something has called out of somewhere. Something in me is trying to answer.... Oh, these men, this Group of Seven, what have they created? ... What language do they speak, those silent, awe-filled spaces? I do not know. Wait and listen; you shall hear by and by .... (pp. 6–7)

During her time with them, she asked the group, particularly Lawren Harris, to explain their philosophy of art, their techniques, and their way of working. She compared their experience to her own struggles and to her ongoing search to reveal on canvas a deep connection to nature. She recognized that such an exchange of ideas and techniques had been missing in her solitary practice, but seeing the Group of Seven's work sharpened her understanding of her own process and made her eager to return to her studio, clearer now about what she wished to achieve. "When will I start to work?" she asked. "Lawren Harris's pictures are still in my brain. They have got there to stay. I don't believe anything will oust them. I hope not because they make my thoughts and life better" (p. 19).

Over the next few years, Emily worked intensely and decisively to realize her vision, including journaling as a regular and important part of this process:

> Yesterday I went to town and bought this book to enter scraps in, not a diary of statistics and dates and decency of spelling and happenings but just to jot down in, unvarnished me, old me at fifty-eight—old, old, old, in most ways and in others just a baby with so much to learn and not much time left …. it helps to write things and thoughts down …. I want my thoughts clear and straight for my work. (p. 20)

And later she wrote: "Trying to find equivalents for things in words helps me find equivalents in painting. That is the reason for this journal. Everything is all connected up" (p. 22).

Her process was much larger than simply going into the woods with a sketchpad and some paints. Rather this work was multifaceted and encompassed her whole life, even its daily events. She walked her dogs and considered how she would paint the sea and forest; she read a book and drew connections between the ideas and her art. She found that she even dreamt her painting:

> Last night I dreamed that I came face to face with a picture I had done and forgotten, a forest done in simple movement, just forms of trees moving in space. That is the third time I have seen pictures in my dreams, a glint of what I am striving to attain. (p. 25)

She continued her correspondence with Lawren Harris, discussing issues about their work. "They were the first real exchanges of thought in regard to work I had ever experienced," she noted. "They helped wonderfully. He made many things clear, and the unaccustomed putting down of my own thoughts in black and white helped me to clarify them and to find out my own aims and beliefs" (p. 21).

Using her journal, she maintained a dialogue with herself as well, questioning what she was trying to understand and represent: "I'm always asking myself the question, What is it you are struggling for? What is that vital thing the woods contain, possess, that you want? Why do you go back and back to the woods unsatisfied, longing to express something that is there and not able to find it?" (pp. 28–29). Sometimes, she seemed to speak directly to the work that engaged her:

> It is D'Sonoqua on the housepost up in the burnt part, strangled round by undergrowth. I want the pole vague and the tangle of growth strenuous. I want the ferocious, strangled lonesomeness of that place, creepy, nervy, forsaken, dank, dirty, dilapidated, the rank smell of nettles and rotting wood, the lush green of the rank sea grass and the overgrown bushes, and the great dense forest behind full of unseen things and great silence, and on the sea the sun beating down, and on the sand, everywhere, circling me, that army of cats, purring and rubbing, following my every footstep. (p. 6)

In these journal pages, she directed her efforts to the interpretation of the spirit of creation through painting. For Emily, as for many successful artists, the drive was to represent a moment of being fully present in life. She reminded herself:

> Do not try to do extraordinary things but do ordinary things with intensity. Push your idea to the limit, distorting if necessary to drive the point home and intensify it, but stick to the one central idea, getting it across at all costs. Have a central idea in any picture and let all else in the picture lead up to that one thought or idea. Find the leading rhythm and the dominant style or predominating form. (p. 32)

Her aesthetic practice intertwined with the other aspects of her life— daily work, friends and family, and engagement with other art forms and the work of others—to create a rich emotional landscape. Emily Carr understood how careful attention to the interpretive work of living enriched the interpretive work of her art.

> I begin to see that everything is perfectly balanced so that what one borrows one must pay back in some form or another, that everything has its own place but is interdependent on the rest, that a picture, like life, must also have perfect balance. Every part of it also is dependent on the whole and the whole is dependent on every part. (p. 61)

Emily Carr searched for what she had not yet seen and sought out what she did not know to challenge what she had accomplished and to help her move closer to what she envisaged painting. She juxtaposed many different experiences with her work so that she could understand more deeply and imagine more sharply the art she was creating.

Carr was an artist in a dialogic community—with other painters, with her journal. Having finally found a way of articulating her vision, she was able to accomplish the most significant work of her career. With new techniques, texts, and ideas juxtaposed to her previous experiences, she was able to interpret those interactions for new learning and insight.

It occurred to me, in studying this time in Carr's life, that her experience of participating in the interpretive structures of a collective rather than being isolated and marginalized as she often was in her early work had important parallels to some of the processes I was seeing in the writers' groups. The consciousness toward language, the attuning of rhythm, and the exploration of the stories' meanings seemed to flourish in such a setting where conversations were often rich and exciting.

Using Carr's work as a focus, this chapter explores the possibilities of aesthetic practice within dialogic and group structures to understand the influence of the collective on writing. I begin with a closer examination of one subject of Emily's work and then describe my own interpretive dialogue with her. From there, I move to explore in more detail the interpretive practices in writing groups, describing how the rhythms, question of language and experimentation with structures evolved, ending with a consideration of why such collectives are important for this work.

The D'Sonoqua Works of Emily Carr

Before Emily traveled to meet the Group of Seven, she had lived through fifteen years where she claimed not to have painted anything at all—at least, she thought, nothing of significance. She had been in France where she learned techniques of modern French painting, but had also spent much of that time in ill health. Back in Victoria, she opened a boarding house to make ends meet and the need to earn a living consumed her. For Emily, those were dark and bitter years with very little time for painting and art.

Her trip to Toronto, however, interrupted her isolation and her stifling self-pity. Entirely new possibilities opened up for her in the conversations with the other artists and these began to shape her conception of what she had been struggling to paint. She heard for the first time about theosophy, a philosophy that draws on traditions from both the East and West, emphasizing the spiritual richness of the environment and the role of the artist in expressing an inner life. She had not considered ideas of the spirit outside Christianity, and she was astonished to see their manifestation in the paintings, particularly in Lawren Harris' work. Much of his art "could be thought of as expressions fulfilling theosophic principles. Their emphasis on light as a primary means of expression related to the clear white light of theosophic symbolism representing eternal truth prior to its splitting into self-asserting colours" (Shadbolt, 1990, p. 69).

As well as the philosophic and spiritual principles that guided him, Harris told Emily about the painting techniques that helped him achieve the energy of such lifeforce in his landscapes. She noted in her journal: "Mr. Harris showed me the different qualities he put in his paint to give vibration. He often rubs raw linseed oil on to the canvas and paints into that, and he oils out his darks, when they sink in, with retouching varnish" (p. 16).

At last Emily had an opportunity to speak about her deep spiritual connection to nature and to translate such an understanding through painting. As Doris Shadbolt noted in her exploration of the themes in Emily's work, this innate religious trait was a guiding force in the decisions that led to her artistic expression even though the link may not have been consciously made until she met the Group of Seven circle. "The Group," Shadbolt wrote, "in providing her with the basic philosophical-spiritual construct in which her mature painting would be grounded, was crucial to her resurgence" (p. 66).

The juxtaposition of these experiences and conversations enabled Emily to reinterpret her work and to realize how she could symbolize these understandings onto canvas. Such work for her was a deeply sensual engagement of memory, emotion, and insight.

> Do not forget life, artists. A picture is not a collection of portrayed objects nor is it a certain effect of light and shade nor is it a souvenir of a place nor a sentimental reminder, nor is it a show of colour nor a magnificence of form, nor yet is it anything seeable or sayable. It is a glimpse of God interpreted by the soul. It is life to some degree expressed. (p. 57)

In the three years or so following her meeting with the Group of Seven, one can see the shift in Emily's work beginning. While she had long painted West Coast Aboriginal themes and subjects, her early work in this area seems anthropological, more a faithful reproduction of what Carr saw as a rapidly disappearing way of life. Her paintings during the early years of the 1930s, however, began to show an intermingling of her understanding of Aboriginal mythology and her feeling about nature. For example, in her 1931 painting *Vanquished*, there are signs of a disappearing race of Zuoqua but also the expressiveness of the landscape with its heavy hanging clouds and vertical bursts of light upon a land seemingly in upheaval. She worked to express the play of light, shadow, color, and form in the forest, trying to create an emotional landscape exuding energy and spirit.

Some of her more interesting work from this time were her paintings of D'Sonoqua, a legendary woman from Kwakiutl myth representing the dark side of maternal instinct that was threatening instead of nurturing to children. Emily described her first vision of this sculpture:

> She seemed to be part of the tree itself, as if she had grown there at its heart, and the carver had only chipped away the outer wood so that you could see her.... Now I saw her face. The eyes were two rounds of black, set in wider rounds of white, and placed in deep sockets under wide, black eyebrows. Their fixed stare bored into me as if the very life of the old cedar looked out, and it seemed that the voice of the tree itself might have burst from that great round cavity, with projecting lips, that was her mouth.... The rain stopped, and white mist came up from the sea, gradually paling her back into the forest. It was as if she belonged there, and the mist were carrying her home. Presently the mist took the forest too, and, wrapping them both together, hid them away. (1951, p. 33)

Emily wrote about her emotional response to the carving, using personal narrative to interpret the strong expression of this art form. This view of art had been "opened up for her by her contact with Harris and the other easterners. They had substantiated her interest in native art and had enabled her to identify virtues in it that related to her vision of art" (Shadbolt, p. 115).

Another experience with a D'Sonoqua, quoted from Emily's journal earlier, was equally as mysterious and mystical for her. She had come across a village that was deserted except for a collection of cats that followed her and gathered at her feet for her two days of sketching. In the painting, *Zunoqua of the Cat Village,* Emily represented the eeriness through the heads and eyes of cats emerging from here and there on the canvas in a surreal and disjointed fashion. In her second painting of this D'Sonoqua, *Strangled by the Growth,* she reverted to the more fearful image of a figure that "glares malevolently through the writhing, semi-abstract bands of foliage" (Blanchard, 1987, p. 226).

The emergence of this threatening female figure in the forest was a catalyst for Emily to interpret the contradictory feelings of nurturing and threat that exist in each moment. These paintings also seemed to be a transition for her, a bridge between her more realistic representation of Aboriginal life and her greater focus on the forest with its own mythic mysticism. In the years following, this focus on the character of the land would texture Emily's interpretations.

The D'Sonoqua haunted Emily with feelings of both attraction and repulsion for the figure. In *Klee Wyck* she wrote: "I never went to that village again, but the fierce wooden image often came to me, both in my waking and in my sleeping" (1951, p. 34). I wondered if her fascination with D'Sonoqua also represented some of her contradictory attitudes toward being female. Using Carr's own words about her experience with D'Sonoqua as well as the paintings, I juxtaposed my own interpretations to write the following poem:

D'Sonoqua, Woman Of The Woods

Each mask took on the life
and spirit of the persona
it represented. Dzunuk'wa
took on the spirit of womanhood
gone mad, one who defied
the most primal maternal
instinct to protect children
and instead threatened them.

— Chief Robert Joseph, *Gwawa'enuxw tribe*[1]

she massaged
from great cedar bole
smoothed soothed
from beneath wood chips
her heavy red trunk

cradle for words
and children
she wraps within her

the tree voice sighs
from her dark
mouth cave
calling for poems
enchanting

wide black brows over
deep white sockets cup
her eyes round
watch tongue
for slip and
one of the children

eagle-headed breasts
fiercely carved
pierce suckling mouth
stop words

arms spliced from trunk
flung wide entice
those who dare draw near
listen
cries of children

I never went
to that village again,
but the fierce
wooden image
often came to me,
both in my waking
and in my sleeping

> – Emily Carr, *Klee Wyck*

(Luce-Kapler, 2003, pp. 26–27)

Interpretation is essential to the creative process. In interpreting, we attend to details and translate them into a different register or medium. The process interrupts the present form of the subject matter and realizes new connections, new visions, and another set of relations. The paintings of D'Sonoqua became an opportunity for me to juxtapose the visual with texts and explore Emily's sense of being female and to see my own experience and that of other women differently.

The contradiction that I recognized in this aspect of Emily's work was a theme that reappeared many times in my journal. I had begun this project by wishing to explore Emily Carr's life in depth, to write poetry and prose that interpreted my impressions of her work as an artist and writer. When I recognized the contradictions between us, I felt I had to write about those. There was no way of standing back and observing and speculating on her life without feeling mine bumped up against hers: prairie to temperate rainforest.

I had begun by recording details of Emily's life—her birth and baptism, her thoughts about her family, her imaginings—but the record-keeping felt plodding and tedious; I did not know what I was accomplishing. Then, after a week of this, there was an entry in my journal: *I think the way I am going to write this is to find some parallels to my life.* This recognition shifted the entries from biographical details to observations about our lives:

> Her writing style in her biography is most unusual at times … she can cover times and events with rapid swiftness that necessitates my rereading a section and at other times she can give the most minute detail so that I wonder how her memory can reconstruct that so vividly. But then in some ways I think my memory works the same. I remember sensory detail with sometimes excruciating clarity and then want to speed through events associated with that image. My voice and stories are reflected off hers as hers are off mine and there is an echoing and an answering at work here. I see the piece being one of voices speaking in different ways and telling a story of being a woman and being an artist … knowing this, I have a focus for what I want to do … I think I would like to use some of my poetry/stories in answer to her

paintings/writing. I am getting a sense of power building here. Of two voices speaking back and forth while other voices enter the conversation. I am enjoying this process more now that it has begun or that I have recognised that it has begun.

Early pieces of my poetry began to establish our two voices— voices that would continue to energise the work. Initially, I placed the two speakers in their own stanzas on either side of the page; this writing was tentative and reluctant to cross boundaries. I perhaps was resisting the possibility that involving myself in this conversation might raise difficult questions and pose interesting challenges for me.

Nevertheless, opening up to her voice and speaking in return seemed to be the only way I would come to have a deeper appreciation for her work. As I read her journals and stories and examined her paintings, I found myself growing impatient at times with her attitudes; I felt annoyed with her opinions. Other times, I was left breathless with her insight. Often I would have to stop reading or looking just to find some equilibrium. She was challenging the difficult bits of my life, and this discomfort initiated some of the best dialogues, spanning a passion for artistic work to the demands placed upon a female artist such as the following piece from my journal. My writing in italics is juxtaposed with excerpts from Emily's published journal, *Hundreds and Thousands.*

I feel out-of-sorts. For two or three days now. A cork on water, leaves on the wind. Aimless, wrung out. I don't want to sit at my computer; I don't know how to start. There is a disconnection, my phone call keeps getting the busy signal. I'm afraid of losing the writing … It is my breath.

I do not understand this great obstinacy, wanting and won't all in the same moment. Seems as though I am chained up and have to wait to be loosed, as though I got stage fright, scared of my own self, of my blindness and ignorance (p. 263). This morning an artist of Budapest visited me. He found my work more like a man's than a woman's. He thinks women find it harder to separate things from themselves, to forget themselves in their work, to concentrate (1966, pp. 237–238).

Writing time is derelict time in some ways to me—stolen, sneaky, precious times, hiding just to be with the writing. It is fine to say that the writing should take precedence above all else and that I should devote my life to it, but I have teaching, children, a husband.

I am always asking myself the question, What is it you are struggling for? What is the vital thing the woods contain, possess, that you want? Why do you go back and back to the woods unsatisfied, longing to express something that is there and not able to find it? (pp. 28–29)

I think that writing is so important to my idea of myself and how I relate to the world that I haven't touched it for a few days. There is a sense of distance and a fear that I will lose it. There is a side of me that longs for the comfort of knowing that I will always be able to write, that I can always do it. At the same time, there is this edge of desperation that puts a bite in my writing and I don't want to lose that.

Through this talking back and forth, the writing began to move from dialogues to poems where I embodied the ideas through the imagery. My responses to Emily began to encompass an understanding of the pattern of relationship between us and of the multi-voiced nature of such a dialogue.

Dark Moon

I don't know sometimes where I end and you begin.
    I watch you writing notes in your sketchbook,
    become poem of your seeing as my fingers soften
    into brushes painting seasalt rainforest.

Last night I wrote about working with my mother in
    her kitchen until it was you slicing apples instead
    of me, asking for the chicken pie recipe that baked
    in the woodstove steam misting double-hung
    windows clouding the raspberry patch beyond the
    garden thick with summer flowers.

The squat fridge hummed to the thump of the rolling
    pin smoothing my mother's arms into dough as she

invited you for supper clearing a place at the grey
formica table for fresh fruit and Jersey cream.

My flesh heavy with your longing, I don't recognize the
turn of ankle or curve of hips. I wonder where you
are waiting, listen for your fading voice. In my eyes
are landscapes condensed in a Claude glass
the chiaroscuro of a raspberry moon.

(Luce-Kapler, 2003, p. 25)

My dialogues with Emily Carr brought me into a new conversation and helped me understand the work that I was doing with the
women writers more clearly. I could see how the moments of our
lives, entangled in many relationships, could take shape through aesthetic practice—in our case writing—and how such practice offered
a new eye on our sense of subjectivity. Who I was in the world
shifted through my deepening awareness of the threads of connection among my associations with others, my reading and writing of
texts, my lived experience—through all the aspects of my existence.
My sense of writing also shifted. I was clearer about the processes in
which I engaged and their effects; I developed a greater appreciation
for the intellectual and emotional power of such a practice.

As Emily noted in her journal, interpretive structures are important. Her meetings with practicing artists brought her into a new
conversation, shifting her understanding through exposure to a different language and process when Harris introduced her to theosophy and showed her some of his techniques to give paint a new
vibrancy. Her aesthetic and spiritual engagements with the Group
of Seven revealed her own desires for art, including leading her to
understand that her inspiration lay not in theosophy, but rather in the
deeper understanding it brought to her Christianity. The tension between her old way of working and understanding and these new ideas
brought her to look more deeply at what she was representing through
her art as her description of dreams and her assessments of her
sketches and paintings reveal in the journal. She was bringing together

the connections between her reflections, her life, and her imaginings. As she noted: "find the threads, loose them again perhaps and pick them up again and again till you don't see the threads but the tightly woven fabric that forms a complete nest" (1966, p. 181).

Through my conversations with Emily, I was able to weave a picture of my work as a writer and thread those insights to my work in writing groups.

Interpretive Practices in Writing Groups

The conversations in the women's writing groups, the interpretive practices that we shared, and the opportunities we had to consider each other's writing and to co-create some pieces and performances brought richness to our interpretations of experience. Many of the women were able to take risks with the subject matter and even make some radical changes, such as Carmen's separation from her husband. They could see things differently through writing and having that writing read and discussed.

A number of activities and structures enabled such interpretations. Most importantly, perhaps, was the creation of a group as a location where one could express her opinion and feel heard. Nelle Morton, a social activist and theologian, has explored the power of groups for women in reinterpreting their experience—what she called being "heard into speech."

> Yet, the new words and the new way old words came to expression, while in the context of history, were not evoked by history. Neither oppression nor suffering shaped their speech. Women came to new speech simply because they were being heard. Hearing became an act of receiving the woman as well as the words she was speaking. (1985, p. 17)

When women have the opportunity to speak or write in language that expresses their being, the authenticity of the experience is engaging even when it may be disturbing and disruptive. Within such a space, women can engage in dialogues—both with themselves and others—and through such a process new ways of being and doing are shared and created. Engaging in an aesthetic practice within such a space deepens the opportunity to explore this speaking and hearing into being.

One of my most recent groups focused on examining some of the practices that had seemed so productive with my earlier writing groups. During those previous occasions, I focused on the responses of the women through writing and their understanding of subjectivity. This time, I wanted to work with the structure of the writing activities and develop some new possibilities.

The group, composed of three graduate students—Marie, Aline and Sarah—met regularly with me for a term. The women had not had much experience with writing anything beyond essays since they left high school. They were eager to develop their skills in preparation for working with undergraduates in my writing project, but they also felt some trepidation since it had been so long since they had even tried to write fiction or poetry.

As a way of preparing for the writing groups the women would be leading, we developed an interpretive process. I wanted writers to explore one incident through three different forms because I felt that experimenting with different techniques of writing would bring them to new interpretations about the incident—just as Emily Carr's exposure to new processes of painting brought her new realizations.[2] At the same time, I wanted us to explore ideas that would feed our writing and so provided several pieces for reading, including the book *Seven Life Lessons of Chaos* that in part described the relationship between chaos theory, creativity, and working collectively.

We began by writing narratives about an incident in our lives since that genre was the most familiar. Marie wrote about an experience with a parent in a Colombia where she taught in an International school. Aline described a haunted house where she had lived, explaining several mysterious incidents that had happened to her family. Sarah wrote about her work with a young man who had been diagnosed with learning disabilities. As I expected, we all wrote in first person, describing the details we felt were most important to the event.

My narrative described the last days of my grandmother's life twenty years ago. As she lay dying in the hospital, my mother and I cleaned out her room at the nursing home, sorting through the final treasures and detritus of her life. One of the treasures that my mother gave me were four needlepoint pictures:

> After helping me unload the chair, my mother reaches into one of the boxes and hands me four of Vantie's needlepoint. Two are pink roses on a cream background; the other two are a boy and girl with toys— the boy with a dog and wagon, the girl with a doll and carriage—each against a grey background. They have hung in my grandmother's house ever since she finished them in the early sixties. I can remember her working on them, having them framed, hanging them. They are exactly what I want.

This brief summary elides many of the details of the family response to her death developed in the narrative, but reflects the tone of my piece, which was similar to the others' narratives.

We discussed the process and the narratives in detail at our next meeting, aiming to illustrate the event as clearly as we could. As we talked about each one, it was obvious that there was deep emotional attachment to these stories and that the words on the page carried the weight of frustration, fear, joy, and sadness. Through our focus on the texts, we came to know each other much better and to understand the significance of the work for each person. We all seemed to have moments of surprise, too, when someone's observation or our recognition of a word used, helped us to understand our own relationship to the incident. The narratives became a location for deeper conversation; they gave us entry into talking about ideas and feelings that may not have arisen in any other context.

When we felt that the narratives were finished, the next task was to turn them into a poem. This process proved to be more difficult because the women's experience with poetry was even less than with other forms of writing. Marie told us that her memories of poetry focused on Shakespeare's sonnets, some of which she had to memorize. Years later she was still able to recite them, realizing that she did not know their meaning.

When she studied poetry in university, her experience did not enrich her understanding of what she thought was supposed to be a beautiful form of expression. She could not get past the underlying message that there was always a correct interpretation of the poem and one had to work to discover it.

Her fondest memory of poetry in school arose from an independent study of Leonard Cohen where she tried to imitate his writing style. She experimented, reading his poems the way she wanted to and writing some of her own in response. When she presented her project, she described her huge feeling of risk even though everything went well. "That's the last time I can remember writing a poem," she said. "I feel a bit 'ripped off' … I don't know the language well enough to articulate clearly what it is that I feel has happened, I just know that I have been cheated. There definitely is more to poetry than what I was taught."

Aline remembered her opportunities for writing in school as being very limited. She explained: "I spent most of my time trying to figure out how to get the best marks. For example, I did my O-levels in English literature and English language. I remember the creative question on the latter being based on the title "The Bend in the Road" (we had to write a narrative that would suit the title). The other component was to summarize an article. So much for creativity! For two years, all we did in class was talk about what might be on the exam, and practice for that and get the best marks."

In my experience with poetry—writing and teaching it as well as being taught—an effective way to begin a poem is to use other poems as an exercise. In keeping with our focus on research in the group, I chose several of Laurel Richardson's (1997) collection of nine poems, which are an interpretation of data from her research about marriage and the family. For example, one of the poems reads as follows:

LULLABY

Time	When he was a baby,
goes	I wondered if he
slowly	would die in his sleep,
thinking	in my sleep.
about	
dying	
giving	
me	
more	
time	
to	
think	Joe said it didn't matter
about	Death, he said, is best
dying	after a good night's sleep.

(p. 176)

The writers described how much information they could discern through the nine poems juxtaposed over several pages and how fruitfully the gaps spoke about connection and disconnection in marriage and family relationships. Although detailed descriptions of Richardson's participants were not available, we could understand the complexity of those relationships she had found in her data.

Using the idea of grouping several poems around a similar theme, the writers felt they could describe the most telling moments of their experience by creating several poems following Richardson's structures. By arranging these poems in a sequence, they could see the fine traces of connection among those moments. As readers of the poems, we noticed that we could relate our own interpretations within such a context. The poems seemed more open than the stories, pointing toward the systems of which they were a part.

One of my poems based on the narrative used the very short lines inspired by Richardson's poem above. By focusing on a simple structure, I was able to think about the emotional heart of my piece,

which was the image of my grandmother in the hospital near death
and the memories associated with that time.

Memory

Curled
fetus
of light
swimming
in thickness

Parchment
fingers
touch
silver frame
imagine
playmate

Planting
gardens
in 1950
calendar
pages
of forgetting

Ironing
paisley
tailored
waist
green
buttons

Reluctant
ending

Immaculate
forgetfulness

This technique of writing created some interesting interpretations among the group. We described how poetry invited us to pay attention to what is important and to choose our details carefully. By seeing the incident expressed in another form, the rhythm of the event was sometimes clearer as were the most important elements of the memory, such as with my poem. The distillation brought a new understanding to each incident. Sarah found Richardson's poetic techniques so helpful in understanding her writing that she went on to report some of the data in her thesis through poetic structures. Particularly evocative were her representations of the young man's voice describing his life with learning disabilities. The rhythms of his speech and the imagery of his experience were brought to life within the academic text. As Melisa Cahnmann stated in her argument for the use of poetry in research:

> In educational research and practice we are working with human beings in all their ever-changing complexity. Incorporating the craft, practice, and possibility of poetry in our research enhances our ability to understand classroom life and support students' potential to add their voices to a more socially just and democratic society. (2003, p. 34)

In our discussions about how different forms shifted and influenced interpretation, we also explored the influence of the group structure on our work. Part of these conversations included our reading of the Briggs and Peat book, which provided new language for talking about the qualities of collective work through the lens of chaos theory. Briggs and Peat suggested:

> As individuals—each with their own self-organized creativity—couple together, some degrees of freedom are given up but other degrees are discovered. A new collective intelligence emerges, an open system, unpredictable from anything one could have expected by observing the individuals acting in isolation. (1999, p. 67)

We certainly had the sense that the group had developed a way of conversing, writing, and reading that influenced each of us. Suggestions for rewriting were woven into the stories and poems. Images that we shared appeared in different contexts. And our questions seemed particularly perceptive because an understanding of the other's experience had developed through the writing and conversation. For instance, because we had first read and closely discussed Marie's narrative of teaching in Colombia, we were able to ask her why she had chosen some images from that experience and omitted others in her poem. By making decisions about what had to remain in the poem, Marie found she touched on the emotional center of that incident. In our conversation with her, she had the opportunity to reflect on that process and realize a new interpretation of that experience—that of important cultural differences. Her realization of this theme influenced her thesis research and formed an important aspect of that work.

For a semester, we discussed our readings (Briggs and Peat as well as other books we were reading individually) and the research in which each of us was engaged. Throughout, we returned again and again to the central story which we had written as a narrative and a poem. Those stories became a focal point through which we understood our other reading and work. They also served to create a conversation that was particular to our group—one that would not be readily comprehensible to an outsider. Such a conversation influenced the particular character of the group as we shared language, rhythms and sense of space. I compared this particular sense of group character to Bakhtin's conception of chronotopes.

Developing a sense of time-space from Einstein's work, Bakhtin was interested in how all contexts are shaped by the kind of time and space that operates within them. Time and space vary in qualities, he suggested, and different activity and representations of those activities presume different kinds of time and space. "Time, as it were, thickens, takes on flesh, becomes artistically visible; likewise, space becomes charged and responsive to the movements of time, plot and history" (1981, p. 84).

While Bakhtin primarily focused on chronotopes as they functioned in literature, he also recognized that the sense of space and time in lived experience served as the source for literary representation. He noted that organisms relied on a variety of rhythms that differed from each other and from those of other organisms. "Furthermore, different social activities are also defined by various kinds of fused time and space: the rhythms and spatial organization of the assembly line, agricultural labor, sexual intercourse, and parlor conversation differ markedly" (Morson & Emerson, 1990, p. 368).

Like the heteroglossia, these chronotopes of living interact dialogically, what Bakhtin called "heterochrony." In the group, each woman came with her own particular sense of time and space, her own chronotope, as well as that of her writing, which offered a subjunctive space and time of possibility. Through interaction with others, these chronotopes co-created a group space and time.

Creating new spaces and time for writing—either individually or within a group—widens the possibilities, but also can increase the sense of risk as I described with Carmen's experience. Conversations with the girls revealed that they were dealing with issues of risk and safety with the spaces of writing as well.

Sophia told us that "some of my poems I'm going to write about something that I feel or about this other person whatever and someone's going to read it or I'm afraid someone else is going to read it. So I don't—that's another reason why I don't write. I write in my mind like whenever I'm walking to school or whatever."

Alexis elaborated with some of her difficulties writing. "Sometimes I have time for writing. I go through spurts. Sometimes I write three times a day. I just write when I feel like it like two in the morning. Then I'm tired the next day …. I have a book that I carry around with me. I feel tormented a lot of the time though. Because I can't say what I mean and I can't get it out. And it always seems stupid to me and then my friends read it."

Genevieve also described similar experiences. "Whenever I pick up the pen, whatever I'm thinking I distort it and it comes out on the page all wrong. And then I go back and read it and I go this is what I'm feeling. You know. How do you put it into words?"

Perhaps groups and writing practices offer some way of beginning, a metaphorical cave where we can begin to communicate what we alone imagined. The group develops a particular character that, if it is working, establishes space for creation. For writing groups, because texts are part of their focus, the workings of textuality contribute to this collective, in particular the effects of intertextuality.

The Intertextuality of the Group

In my experience as a writer and with my research into writing, I often confront the notion of the individual versus the group. While those involved in textual productions agree that collaboration during the process can be valuable, the attribution of the final product is usually to an individual or, at most, several co-authors. For instance, writing teachers and researchers have long supported the use of collaborative groups to facilitate the development of writing skills and fluency. The claims of such studies range from an improvement in revision skills and greater capability with language and style to a better sense of audience and community (see e.g., Bruffee, 1984; Elbow, 1973; Macrorie 1970; Moffett, 1968; Murray, 1985), but when that process is over, the marking generally focuses on individual production.

In *Teaching the Universe of Discourse,* James Moffett noted that in learning to write, the "most critical adjustment one makes is to relinquish collaborative discourse, with its reciprocal prompting and cognitive cooperation, and go it alone" (1968, p. 87). In response, Ede and Lunsford observed,

> the composition theorists and teachers most often identified with collaborative learning and peer response techniques—James Moffett, Donald Murray, Peter Elbow, Ken Macrorie—are also usually identified with Bizzell's 'inner-directed' group or Berlin's 'expressionist' group, which posit the uniqueness of individual imagination and see writing as a means of expressing an autonomous self. Ironically, then, the very writers most often associated with collaborative learning hold

implicitly to traditional concepts of autonomous individualism, authorship, and authority for texts. (1990, p. 113)

Spigelman (1998), in her study of textual ownership in peer writing groups, illustrated how these tensions between the public and the private play out by opening with a quotation from a student's journal: "I like the writing groups, but I don't use the advice because then the paper would not be *my own*. I feel that my writing is *my writing* and should not be based upon what advice is given by others" (Spigelman's added emphasis, p. 234).

With such deeply ingrained cultural beliefs about authorship and how it represents self-expression (*my own; my writing*), it is not surprising that most discussions about writing groups foreground benefits for the individual. Writer Margaret Atwood criticized this perspective: "Readers and critics both are addicted to the concept of self-expression, the writer as a kind of spider, spinning out his entire work from within. This view depends on a solipsism, the idea that we are all self-enclosed monads, with an inside and an outside, and that nothing from the outside ever gets in" (1982, p. 342).

Foucault described how, in writing and publishing, individualism created conditions for the concept of author to emerge thereby allowing the work to be attributed to one person who could be held responsible. Such designations subjected textual practices to regulation and constraint, including stopping the proliferation of meaning:

> the author is not an indefinite source of significations which fill a work; the author does not precede the works; he is a certain functional principle by which, in our culture, one limits, excludes, and chooses; in short, by which one impedes the free circulation, the free manipulation, the free composition, decomposition, and recomposition of fiction. (Foucault, 1984, p. 119)

With this construction of "author," the writer could be encouraged to modify or restrain his or her text. The privileging of individual production makes it difficult to acknowledge the contributions of a collective to one's writing, especially when marks or publication is at stake. If we take another look, however, at the processes of textual creation, the role of collaboration is more evident, especially when we consider the phenomenon of intertextuality.

Claudio Guillén (1993) has offered a useful description. He suggested that literary work is "heterotextual" (p. 245), calling into question the notion of "original work," which implies that one can discover the "true" origins of a text or that the work arises from the author without any precedence. In an effort to show the complex effects of other texts and textual practices on literature, Guillén drew from Kristeva's conception of intertextuality. She described a dialogue within the text that takes place among "three languages: that of the writing subject, that of the addressee (whether outside or inside the work), and that of exterior texts, or cultural context, present or past," (Guillén, p. 245) giving texts a dynamic and heterogeneous nature. Guillén further developed this idea of intertextuality to involve "horizontal" and "vertical" readings.

The horizontal effect of intertextuality describes the practice of evoking past texts, authorities or styles without these elements intervening decisively in the semantic structure. Guillén calls this reading "citation" (p. 251). In writing this chapter, for instance, my reference to Guillén's work brings an important perspective to my work but does significantly alter the structures I am using to create meaning. A vertical reading, on the other hand, what he calls "significance," does affect the semantic structure. Unlike the citation axis, the intertexuality of significance mingles words, themes and contexts with the writer's intentions and thus is less attributable to specific sources. For example, intertextuality that affects a poem vertically begins to blur the boundaries between the "fictitious and the natural, the novel and the autobiography, the original and the replicated, the self and the other, written and read, broken and whole" (McHugh, 1993, p. 71). My understanding of Gail Scott's work for instance—that is her blurring of the essay with the poetic—has certainly influenced the juxtaposition of forms and voices that I have used in writing this text. Those influences, however, are not as evident as direct citation. Certainly many other intertextual influences are at work in the semantic structures of my text that I do not even recognize. Intertext, Guillén suggested, reveals the "social aspect of literary writing, whose individual character, up to a certain point, is located at a specific junction of earlier writings" (p. 247).

Within the writing group, this intertextual nature becomes more evident. In one of my recent writing groups composed of English education undergraduates, the writers noticed how the texts of published authors that we read, the work of the others in the group, and the responses to their texts had helped shaped their writing. Most found such a process reassuring not only because the interactions enriched their creative work, but also because their conversations with others helped them discover ways to say more distinctly what they wanted to express, especially the affective threads of their writing. In recognizing how other texts could offer forms and practices for writing and how readers interpret their writing, they developed strategies they planned to use in their writing and teaching beyond the group.

These participants also became more aware of the shared possibilities from which they could draw. One woman talked about the "texture" of the group to describe her tangible sense of relationship and interconnection through shared rhythms, spaces and language. From this ritual of gathering, practices and understandings that developed over time offered a space for taking risks with their texts.

Many of the recent participants, all of whom are teacher candidates, commented on how the group had been the one place where they were able to make sense of their experience, to feel connected to something important, and to share meaningful time with their peers in the midst of a busy year. All of them described the nature of their group in terms beyond themselves and indicated that the group had developed a particular character that influenced their writing in important ways.

Part of the connectedness they were feeling, I believe, came from their awareness of vertical intertextuality. Most of them were aware of citation and referred to other texts and styles in their writing What was less evident to them prior to their work with the group were the influences of those texts and the work of their peers on the semantic structures of their writing. As they wrote about one experience through three different forms—narrative, poetry, and hypermedia—they also became aware of how those forms influenced and changed their understanding of that experience. Within the practices of the group discussions, they noted the collective and emergent qualities of their writing. Most of them believed writing to be a solitary activity when they began the group, but not one left feeling the same way.

In writing groups, then, the importance of what emerges from the conversations, from the texts, and how that dialogue unfolds is as important as the change in the individual writers and their insights about the processes of such creation. Within a company of writers, there is an abundance of language, of rhythm, of vision. When we meet together, reading and writing texts, these creations spill over the edges of our group and bring us closer to the larger circles of literacy in which we live.

Importance of Groups to Writing

During the mid-1990s, I was part of a women's poetry group called, with tongue-in-cheek, "the chix." We met monthly, bringing our poems for close reading and discussion. Of course, the conversation ranged beyond the poems in question to include news about the writing community, to suggest new books to read, and to share the events in our lives. Without conscious awareness, an image that appeared in someone's poem might appear in a totally new context in someone else's. Discussions of rhythm or line breaks about a particular poem would influence other creations in that followed. While each discussion about an individual's work was particular and specific, its details contributed to an overall group conversation about writing and poetry—a conversation that was particular to the group and always emerging.

When I moved away from the city where this group was located, I soon recognized the lack of their feedback and felt my poetry was floundering. While I maintained my practice of reading newly published works in literary magazines and read reviews and while I continued to develop practices for myself, my writing was not developing as it had before. I sometimes found it difficult, too, to analyse my own work. I would know that something was wrong with a poem, but would be unable to discern the problem. I tried communicating with fellow poets through email, and while that was helpful, it was not the same as creating a group, meeting regularly and developing a particular sense of connection. I understood why Emily needed both the communion with other artists and her solitude in the forest to create.

Di Brandt described some of the tensions and discoveries in her collaborative writing projects and how they reminded her of the fluidity of identity and the interplay of "me/not me" that takes place in such work. She challenged the belief that the writer works from a solitary space and explained how working collaboratively illustrated the character of language: "Words being traded back and forth between people, the same words, with slight variations, endless recycling of the same stories and rhythms, each one slightly different from the last, with the transmitter's indelible personal imprint on it, and yet recognizably communal, the same" (1996, p. 82).

In my desire to consider how one might "write otherwise," I see the group interactions as an important aspect to my writing. While writers always draw from the heteroglossia, struggle against centripetal forces and rely on the richness of intertexuality, it is when we can focus on our writing in the company of others that we are more conscious of these processes. When reading to others, seeing our audience respond and participating in interpretations and collective practices, the potential for these productive processes seems greater. In such a setting, one becomes more aware of those processes and systems as she has the opportunity to explore them with others. We participate in a literate community, contributing to it as well as drawing from it. Working in a writing group hones our awareness of the relationship to this community.

Even when we work in isolation, our texts generally are intended for others to read and that sense of the collective to which we send our writing is ever present. The writing group makes the connections concrete and brings new ideas and processes that shape and challenge our thinking. Furthermore, a writing group develops "a new collective intelligence" beyond what any of us can imagine or enact on our own. In chapter 6, I consider how these processes of writing and the work of groups can bring us to "writing otherwise."

Notes

1. Chief Robert Joseph: http://collections.ic.gc.ca/totems/exhibit/kwak/xwintro2.htm
2. The intention was to have narrative, poetry, and hypermedia. With this group, we only explored the first two. It was left to later groups to add the third element.

chapter six

writing otherwise

In other words, how to think, write or read *not* as a woman, but more complexly and less clearly, how to think, write and read otherwise, whether one is a man or woman, how to accommodate issues, qualities, concepts that have not had their time before.

– Elizabeth Grosz

I t is late afternoon toward the end of November. Outside the sky is gray and threatening more cold rain while inside four women gather in a common area, soft chairs pulled together in a close circle, a few incandescent lights glowing instead of the bright fluorescents. Every week for the past two months, they have been meeting, reading theory, bringing writing and talking about the ideas that emerge from such work. They are wondering how the interpretive experience of writing about one event changes when the form of that writing shifts.

Several weeks ago, they each brought narratives they had written about a significant event in their lives. One wrote about inheriting her grandmother's needlepoint, another about a haunting in her family home. The third woman wrote about an experience that she had teaching in Colombia while the fourth described a moment in her research work with a young man who has learning disabilities. They have read and worked on these narratives, sharpening the details and choosing the most evocative. Now they have come to this meeting having turned these incidents into poetry.

The group is more hesitant, uncertain. None of them has written poetry in a long time except for one person. And it's been longer still since most of them have shown anyone their poems. Even in the warm, collective space that they have created, there is a sense of discomfort as they rustle their pages. How does one even begin to talk about one's poem let alone the poems of others?

They hand out their work with apologies: This isn't very good yet. This needs more work. I don't know if I understood how to do this. I had lots of drafts, lots of scratches out.

They begin, choosing a sheet of poems to look at, reading them carefully. Thinking. Then having the author read her work aloud to hear the rhythm. Everyone is familiar with the narrative from which this work has come, but now it seems different. There is an essence of the story here—a swift slide into the heart of it. They talk about the risk in laying it all out on the page. With so few words, it is difficult to hide behind them.

"This is challenging the way I think about words," one says. "But I still feel like I'm looking for my own voice in poetry."

"When you read it out loud," another says, "it brings the feelings closer."

"A poem is like a canvas of feeling," says the third.

"It feels dangerous."

They persist, moving from poem to poem, listening carefully, responding to the experience of hearing the words and reading them on the page. This careful, collective sense-making increases their comfort in learning to talk about each poem, their voices more confident, their bodies softening.

It has taken time to reach this place: time writing first in a more familiar genre; time learning how to speak of writing; time learning how to listen and be silent before responding; time to create an intimate location for poetry.

By shifting their narrative to poetry, they have seen it differently and felt it more closely and deeply. But in raising the affective level of the interpretation, they've also raised their sense of risk. Within such an interpretive space, they suddenly find themselves facing their subjectivity in the company of others.

Reading a Research Moment

I wrote this short descriptive section from notes in my research journal.[1] I am interested in how I immediately noticed the weather, giving importance to the daily unfolding of those patterns as I often do. In part, I believe it is because I grew up on a farm where my father watched the sky for storm clouds, where a thermometer was always perched outside our kitchen window, and where the weather determined our livelihood. Weather became part of my interpretive structures.

Now that I have been paying closer attention to the interpretive processes of writing, I recognize that weather is a consideration especially since the location and situation of the writing does influence the images and rhythms. In the above description, while it is rainy and gray outside as we gather for the meeting, we have turned on incandescent light to offer a warmer glow to the room. Remembering that light, I am aware of how we are in relation to each other: the chairs in a circle, soft and comfortable, our bodies relaxed into the furniture even while there is the bustle and rustle of papers being passed quickly with apologies. In the rhythm of collecting, I remember the sense of habitual practice and can imagine myself back in that room with those women, a tangible sense of that experience warming my body.

I remember other writing groups similarly through the sensory details. Each had its own character, its own atmosphere—a chronotope of collective writing. By looking back at notes or even some of the pieces of writing from those times, I can remember the look of the room or the landscape, the physical presence of the other writers, the emotional texture I felt in the group.

Within this space is both the feeling of safety and of risk. As Di Brandt suggested, writers need the opportunity to leap into the volcano, to explore their real feelings, but they also need a map to get back out. Writing groups can provide such a map through their close attention to the character of language and the intentions of writers.

This microcosmic moment of a writing group points to the importance of recognizing the embodiment of writing, the social influences, and the fluidity of language in defining our subjectivity. How these aspects interact to create a context for writing can be explained if we understand writing as an ecology and recognize the systems of which writing is a part.

In this chapter, I will bring together these aspects of writing to consider its interconnected nature and then explain how understanding in such a way may suggest how we can begin writing otherwise. Our relationship with others in writing groups offers the opportunity to be heard into speech. Through conversation and examination of the texts, writers can become critically aware of their language and through writing practices they can search for new ways of expression. While there is no unifying consciousness for women's or men's writing, there are patterns in its practice that one can see as possibilities for new ways of responding.

The Ecology of Writing

Common images of writers show them stretched out under a tree, their backs propped up against the trunk with notebook in hand or they sit at a desk, fingers flying over a keyboard, surrounded by books. Then there is the famous stereotype of the male writer, shirtsleeves rolled up, pecking at a typewriter, a bottle of whiskey to one side. All these images and many like them have depicted writers. What is often implied in such visions is that most of the writing is internal. We cannot see or understand the mysterious process that creates a rich tapestry of characters and situations.

While there certainly is some truth to those images, they do not portray the awareness writers bring to the life they are representing. They often attend to detail and are close observers; they draw from and frequently revise the tradition of texts that have come before, and they are part of a literate community for whom they write. This connection to the life of textual production embeds the writer in the systems that have influenced and continue to influence writing.

The study of such relationships can be compared to an ecology, a term that came into use when nineteenth century biologists began to study communities of organisms. While scientists developed the term within a biological context, the meaning of ecology has broadened to include the study of other systems. As Capra (1996) pointed out, ecology comes from the Greek *oikos* for household and refers to "the study of relationships that interlink all members of the Earth Household" (p. 32).

In the field of literary theory, as Hayles described, conceptions from science have been evocative descriptions for many of the processes of textual engagement. These conceptions of the world are metaphors that can help us understand other phenomenon in new ways, raising questions and enabling us to understand differently. For instance, in Marilyn Cooper's notion of writing as an ecology, she pointed out that some of the systems that connect writers include those of ideas, purposes, interpersonal interactions, cultural norms and textual forms.

Ecology's ability to focus our attention on a system of relationships is important. While we may think the notion of ecology, usually associated with the natural world, to be far from writing processes, David Abram (1996) has shown the important relationship between language and the more-than-human world. Cooper's understanding of the ecological character of writing stopped with an explanation of human systems; Abram's conception connects us beyond the human.

Relating his own extensive work in ecology and philosophy to the phenomenology of Merleau-Ponty, Abram investigated the roots of language, illustrating its relationship to the natural world. He described the rhythms and textures of our subjective experience, suggesting the importance of paying attention and giving voice to "its enigmatic and ever-shifting patterns" (p. 35). It is easy to ignore or marginalize such experience because it can quickly become part of the fabric of our daily living. Furthermore, western society has privileged and promoted more linear and controlled understandings of experience, making it difficult to see the world as Abram described it: "an intertwined matrix of sensations and perceptions" (p. 39). Humans are both receptors and creators of the world. As we inscribe others (including the non-human) in our experience, so do they inscribe us, weaving "our individual phenomenal fields into a single, ever-shifting fabric, a single phenomenal world or 'reality'" (p. 39).

Meaning is rooted in our bodies. As such, language is not a purely mental phenomenon but is also part of the non-verbal exchange, reflecting the relationship between the semiotic and the symbolic that Kristeva described. Abram detailed language as something living that is continually being remade, woven from the silence that rises from "our perceptual immersion in the depths of an animate, expressive world" (p. 84). He traced the roots of oral language to our responses to the natural sounds about us and then related the development of the alphabet (and thus written language) to its original representation of animals and other natural forms. So, while language and the processes of writing may seem distanced from lived experience, the written word has a potency and a history with the natural world. We are reminded of this through the rhythms of our speech, through the sounds of our language, and with the sensory attention we can access through writing. As Abram noted: "A genuinely ecological approach does not work to attain a mentally envisioned future, but strives to enter, ever more deeply, into the sensorial present" (p. 272).

In thinking of writing as an ecology, then, as I have argued throughout the book, we must bring an attentiveness to such work, an attentiveness that recognizes rhythm, that envisages language as flexible and creative and that understands writing as embedded in a system of relationships with the human and the more-than-human world. With the symbolic, we must remember, there is the semiotic. Ecology was derived from the word for home and habitation, a household as Capra noted. A household is a gathering place, a central location, somewhere to come from and go back to. Whether we consider the home of writing being the individual and her text or the writing group where the text is read or the larger community of readers and writers to which the text is connected, each is a relationship of practices and influences. In what follows, I consider one project that resulted in a poem about American author, Kate Chopin. I begin with a chronological noting of the processes that influenced the writing followed by a reflective section that traces some of the relationships and connections I identify in that process. While I began this work by first identifying the systems that Cooper highlighted, I returned to consider the sensorial aspects of the work as well, remembering Abram's understanding of how writing can embed us in the world.

Kate Chopin

1989: When I was still teaching high school English, a friend who had started teaching at the university gave me a copy of a book listed on her syllabus. It was *The Awakening* by Kate Chopin. I read the slim novella quickly and with some amazement because not more than six months earlier I had rented a movie that told this very story. The title had been different but not the plot or the characters. At the time of watching the movie, I had been very engaged by this story of a woman in the late nineteenth century going against expectations and creating a life for herself that did not depend on the directives of a man. Now that I knew the movie had its basis in a book, I was keen to learn more about the author. This was the first time I had heard of Kate Chopin, but it did not surprise me because during my undergraduate English degree, I remember reading only two women's work: Jane Austen and Charlotte Bronte.

1996: I am a member of a poetry writing group where every two weeks or so, we gather at one of our houses and bring several poems to read. The group reads everyone's work carefully and responds as critical readers. During one of our discussions, someone mentions how the images in a poem remind her of *The Awakening*. It has been several years since I have thought of the novel, but I take it out when I get home and reread it, enjoying the story, the imagery and the rhythm of Chopin's prose as much as I did the first time. The book feels poetic to me.

Later, one of the women in the group sends an email to everyone: "I imagine Edna Pontellier at the end of *The Awakening* swimming and coming toward her is a large row-boat. It is the same boat we are on when we are dreaming. The boat is gray wood, weathered, the edges smooth, hand worn. And all of these hands reach out to her, pull her in effortlessly, row away."

I think about how our discussion of the story and how our work together as women writers is described through her words. We help each other to realize what we are saying through our poems. Instead of drowning, we are brought into a place of support where we are heard and can come to understanding.

May 1, 1999: I have purchased the biography of Kate Chopin and make journal entries as I read it:

> To listen for the voice ... what do I think Kate Chopin's voice sounds like? Kate knew enclosure—the hot steam and the claustrophobia of the south and how things could grow so quickly and encroach on one's territory. There would be little sense of boundaries in terms of self but plenty of boundaries stopping women from wandering outward and moving across the landscape and into whatever parts of society they felt were important.

May 6, 1999: I am thinking about art and boundaries and women. It is a continual fascination. I read about Kate as a child rolled up in a blanket, trying to be invisible so her mother will not see her and punish her yet again for spilling milk across the floor. I remember the image of Emily Carr in the tall grass watching the tiny bug life about her feet and knowing she was safe from anyone's view in the house. Women watching while remaining hidden. I have an image of Edna hiding among the thick draperies of her dining room.

May 18, 1999: My reading and journaling continue: How did I first get drawn in to her, to this obsession with the woman and her vision of seeing the world, the intense claustrophobia of being in a society small as a dark room beneath the stairs, humid air pressing on the heart like the heal of his hand?

I think first it was an obscure movie that no one knew about but that appeared on the shelves of a small Whitecourt video store. Who would have thought that such a thing would appear in a small town in Northern Alberta where there was lumber and oil and not even a movie theatre. Just a couple of video stores, the only opportunity to see movies unless you drove two hours to the big city. Yet here was this small obscure movie about a woman in southern United States who escapes the oppressiveness of the late 19th century society and takes a young lover. Her rebellion finally leads her to despair and the only escape seeming to be drowning in the water. I was enchanted by the mood of that movie, rented it over and over just to be in that place.

How often had I felt constrained by who I was or where I lived? How much of that constraint was who I believed I was or what others believed about me? Looking back, sometimes I think it was a lack of my own imagination not to see doorways—at least compared to Edna Pontellier's life. I could connect with those feelings of suffocation, the sinking down into something that was frightening. I remember when I first read the novel. I was smitten and wanted to learn more. How a woman could write so accurately about oppression. It was nothing like Henry James or D.H. Lawrence. This was how it felt, not how it was perceived. And so I begin.

May 20, 1999: I write the first draft of the poem that eventually becomes the following:

Kate's Edna

Foggy night in autumn. Deep within,
a southern heat and sharp corset.
I watch her white body spill
from the confines of dress, the flash of lightning.
Her hair falls about her shoulders,
shaken loose from the pins. I lift
my own thickness from my neck, loving
the curves of her body
sliding into the waves of the gulf,
her arms outstretched.
She is naked moonlight
polished by late-rising stars,
a wraith upon the water.
She dissolves with every step,
her fingertips, then her arms, smaller
than clam shells across the sand.

> Soon she will slip beneath the surface
> a trail of bubbles marking
> the last of her sighs
> that expect no answer.
> Only the brush of her breath
> will touch cheeks
> of young women longing
> to sing on their own.
>
> (Luce-Kapler, 2000)

July, 2000: I watch another movie version of *The Awakening,* entitled *Grand Isle* with a friend. I explain to him how important this story is to me as it continues to stay with me: a woman who tries to create a space for herself in the world, who awakens, only to find there is no space. The movie seems to capture some of the intensity of the novel and is intriguing. Yet it is not the novel, not the words that entangled me in a vision of steam, heat, and oppression, ending in the cool waters enveloping Edna's body. Still, it brings me back into the story to remember my other Kate poems, to remind me of my attraction to a book written about a woman trying to be otherwise.

December 2002: In gathering the artifacts to tell this story, I am amazed to find all the threads that I do and surprised at how easily I gather them up. This story is clearly a theme for me; that is, it continues to hold deep significance for my life. I am interested in how the work of Kate Chopin and the life of Edna Pontellier continue to appear in mine without my conscious bidding.

The Complexity of Writing

In relaying this small example of one poem, I know I have only the touched the surface of all the connections and influences that might be traced through this experience. Throughout this story, I can read the imprints of the social, cultural and historical constructions of women. In Kate's response to her environment and her description of Edna's suffocating world, one can recognize the boundaries that existed for women during that time and some which remain. How women find space for developing a sense of self fascinates me and suggests why I continue to return to *The Awakening*.

The image of suffocation, both through Edna's drowning and Kate's memory of being wrapped in a blanket as a child, reveal the bodily reaction to the societal constraints. To break through such oppression demanded strong responses: for Edna it meant an opportunity for the sensual awakening into the pleasures of her body while for Chopin it meant creating a stir when she translated some of the work of Guy Maupassant. Much of this work remained unpublished in a climate "where magazines were supposed to preserve the innocence of 'the Young Person.' Maupassant ... had written about parts of the body that did not exist in respectable American fiction, such as thighs and breasts and tongues" (Toth, 1999, p. 159).

One of Chopin's translations included the story about a husband with an erotic obsession for orchards: "their flanks, odorant, and transparent, open for love and more tempting than all women's flesh" (quoted in Toth, p. 160). While such writing clearly influenced Chopin's work, it created some shock among editors.

The sensual richness of life is difficult to contain even through societal constraints. We live in the world through our senses while our language reflects the rhythm of the blood rushing through our veins, the breath that fills our bodies and the shiver along our skin. The rhythm of my poem reflects the slow walk of Edna into the water, the sadness of the moment gathered from the text itself and from the movie interpretations of the moment.

The experience of writing the poem points to the intertexuality of the process: the obvious connection to the novel and the movie versions, the conversations with my writing group and with other women, my experience of feeling suffocated by expectations and so on. All of these possibilities color my language while the words chosen come with their own history of usage such as the word "corset." That image is laden with a history of expectation and oppression for women.

When I reread this interpretation with an awareness of Abram's work, I am surprised that I did not immediately notice all the references to landscape and weather. How easily such qualities become a backdrop for our experience. I am struck by the images of water and humidity that are the physical manifestation of the stifling conditions that drowned Edna and constrained Chopin, who nevertheless responded with the sensual richness of images and language in her writing and translations that challenged the restrained and sterile language of a Victorian era.

I notice the images of water in my poem and in the email from my friend, although in the latter case the water has a restorative quality, reminiscent of Crozier's "birth-gleam," while the rhythms of my poem echo Edna's slow descent into the waves.

My attraction to Chopin's work was likely heightened by the isolation of the small town in which I lived, which was emphasized in my notes. That town was in the midst of a forest where winters seemed long and dark, making the tropical steam of Chopin's world purely imaginary but nevertheless appealing. However, it took a small heat wave in May before I could write Kate's Edna, suggesting to me that my imagination was facilitated by the weather.

It seems clear to me that weather, landscape and the presence of other living beings are richly described and form an important part of the texture of Chopin's work as they did Carr's.

The complexity of this writing event has quickly become apparent even though I have only begun to examine what I am consciously aware of in the creation of this piece. The process I engaged in while writing this one poem drew from several years of experience with the ideas and much thinking about Chopin. This is not to suggest that I knew I was working towards a poem; rather, that in writing, one draws on a wide variety of experiences, times, texts and landscapes.

With this work, I can recognize the participation of the body in the rhythms and images of writing, I can draw attention to some of the social, cultural, and historical influences, and I can use this awareness to question what I have said or not said. All of these aspects influence writing and suggest its ecological character—the household of things in relation.

If we understand this complex and interconnected nature of writing, then there is the possibility for learning how to write otherwise for no system is all-encompassing. As Finke explained: "The intersections, collisions, and perturbations created by the many different agents, institutions, and discourses at work within a society create patterns that cannot be resolved into coherent narratives" (p. 9). This understanding suggests that there are many stories and many ways to tell them and that there is no "women's writing" but rather the possibility to see differently and write with fuller awareness, to write "otherwise."

Writing Otherwise

Complexity theory suggests that the smallest of fluctuations in a system can become amplified to revise patterns and that the results of such disturbances are not readily predictable. Such an understanding offers hope for Grosz's call for "writing otherwise." By working with Irigaray's vision of the future perfect or by bringing new attention to the sensorial quality of language as Abram suggests, the small change, the slight fluctuation could shift the character of the symbolic order.

In my work with women, I have caught glimpses of what writing otherwise might mean. These moments have not been consistent nor sustained; however, within the life of a particular woman, they can change the possibilities that are open for her. The most striking example is Carmen. When she wrote about her life as she understood it unfolding, she saw more clearly what had been happening and what she believed. Writing down her story gave form to the sense of unease and malaise that had been haunting her. She began to reinterpret the choices available and change the direction of her life.

This story and others like it do not suggest a trend in women's writing nor do they get beyond some of the definitions of women and "women's writing." I do think, however, they point to how writing has the potential to create change. Directing our attention to the systems of writing offers new understandings that will shape a different future. For writers and teachers of writing, there are many ways that such attention can be cultivated. In the following sections, I will focus on three approaches I commonly use in my own work and teaching. These approaches help raise awareness of the systems of writing and create productive conditions for such work: (1) introducing writing practices, (2) developing critical awareness, and (3) creating opportunities to be heard into speech.

Writing Practices

I have developed a sense of writing practices from several places. The work of Natalie Goldberg (1986; 1990), who developed her writing practice from Zen Buddhism, became an early inspiration. Goldberg created a series of six rules for writing practice:

1. *Keep your hand moving.* (Don't pause to reread the line you have just written. That's stalling and trying to get control of what you're saying.)
2. *Don't cross out.* (That is editing as you write. Even if you write something you didn't mean to write, leave it.)
3. *Don't worry about spelling, punctuation, grammar.* (Don't even care about staying within the margins and lines on the page.)
4. *Lose control.*
5. *Don't think. Don't get logical.*
6. *Go for the jugular.* (If something comes up in your writing that is scary or naked, dive right into it. It probably has lots of energy.) (1986, p. 8)

These "rules" reminded me of other suggestions by writers, such as W. O. Mitchell's "freefall writing," and I found the invitation to just let language flow onto the page in whatever form is a wonderful way to begin, which is why I refer to this process as "flow writing." I reserved the term "writing practices" for a broader range of possibilities than Goldberg's rules.

This desire to widen the meaning of writing practices relates to my reading of Albert Borgmann (1992) and his explanation of "focal practices," a process that can invite the kind of attention Abram suggested. Borgmann explained that deep engagement with activities such as art making, gardening, or writing bring us to a place of understanding ourselves and our connection to the world. Rather than a singular practice, then, like Goldberg's rules, I have come to think of writing practices as small, focused events that lead people into writing or which help them reinterpret writing.

By creating such structured activities, I have learned that individuals find their ability to write is greater than they thought. Offering a specific focus opens up the possibilities to be what I and two of my colleagues have called "liberating constraints" (Davis et al., 2000); that is, practices that focus our attention in a particular area but leave much room for interpretation.

Writing practices often begin with flow writing or mind mapping, any process that encourages people to write quickly and without thought of constraints such as grammar or logic. This type of writing then becomes the "raw data" for the work in which we will engage. For the young women writers, we would seldom go any further than this, using the "first" writing as a basis for conversation. In most other writing occasions, however, I invite individuals to work with this initial piece to make deeper or different interpretations. These suggestions become the liberating constraints with which they work.

A workshop that I offered several years ago with a group of women offers an example of how writing practices work.

Remembered Rapture

I invited the group of women working with me over the course of a day to engage in a series of writing practices that asked them to explore their relationship to their grandmothers. We began by generating several pieces of writing through different activities and then took one of the pieces through different forms to follow their shifts in understanding and interpretation.

I used the title from a bell hooks' book *remembered rapture* as a way of suggesting a focus for our work. As hooks wrote: "Writing about writing is one way to grasp, hold, and give added meaning to a process that remains one of life's great mysteries. I have not yet found words to truly convey the intensity of this remembered rapture—that moment of exquisite joy when necessary words come together and the work is complete, finished, ready to be read" (1999, p. xvi). hooks described the moment when one has managed to express a memory, an experience, an imagining in a way that seems to capture those moments.

I suggested to the writers that by remembering older women in our lives—grandmothers, biological or otherwise—we would try to feel this sense of rapture in expressing what we had not before and perhaps think about the legacy of these women. hooks appreciated the difficulty in coming to this rapture and I shared her words about the silencing of women's voices and the importance of writing to counteract that: "This precious powerful sense of writing as a healing place where our souls can speak and unfold," hooks wrote, "has been crucial to women's development of a counter-hegemonic experience of creativity within patriarchal culture" (p. 5).

We began by each writing down the name of a woman whom we thought of as grandmother. Then I asked everyone to flow write for fifteen minutes using the writing prompt: "A time I remember with" and the name written on their paper.

Afterward, I brought out my grandmother's button jar. I have used her button jar in many places and situations and the spill of four hundred or so buttons onto a table always invites people into interesting interpretations. I have learned that items that are seemingly simple and commonplace in our lives, such as buttons, often evoke a wealth of memories for writers.

This time was no exception. I started with the story about the button jar, which I have told in other places but bears repeating here[2]:

Since my grandmother's death, her button jar has sat on my shelf: a two-quart sealer like the ones she used for canning dill pickles or carrots or raspberries. As long as I can remember, she loved to sew; she made all her own clothes, many of my grandfather's, and numerous outfits for my sisters and me. The button jar was an important part of that process. If there was one button left on the card when she finished making a dress for me, that button went into the jar just in case. When clothes wore out, she carefully snipped their buttons into the jar before using the cloth for rags. Jackets, dresses, and trousers that were worn long before my birth are remembered in that jar, and when I spin it around, I have memories of moments, impressions, and feelings. The white plastic buttons like the ones my grandfather had on his flannel pyjamas remind me of the nights that he held me to his chest when I was sleepless and afraid until the warmth of the material and his heartbeat lulled me to sleep. I see the green fabric-covered button from the suit my grandmother wore at my uncle's wedding—the one where I was a flower girl and got car sick in my grandfather's new Pontiac StratoChief. Even buttons that I do not recognize remind me of other clothes and other times.

After reading this piece about my grandmother, I spread the buttons onto the table and invited people to choose one and then use it as a prompt to write for ten minutes about the memories it evoked.

At this point, the women had created two pieces of writing: one about a grandmother and another about a memory associated with the button. They were ready to move toward a more interpretive phase of the writing. I asked them to return to their first piece of writing and think of an object and a place that would remind them of their grandmother and to jot it in the margin. Then I asked them to bring together the memory and the grandmother through using the object and the place and discover a relationship among them—either real or imagined—and write a short narrative.

Afterward, I divided the women into smaller groups and asked them to read their narratives to one another. I suggested listeners not critique the work as if it were being marked or judged but rather comment on images that were evocative or ask questions about places where they wanted more information. I wanted the women to feel heard through this experience.

Following the lunch break, I asked them to reinterpret their personal writing into a fictional piece. Moving into such a realm offers new interpretations and sometimes helps individuals read their work quite differently with sometimes surprising insights. To start this process, I handed out copies of pictures depicting older women in various situations. They circulated the pictures and then each woman chose one about whom she would write for fifteen minutes. I told them to write from that character's point of view and gave them some questions to begin answering from that voice either in first or third person: What is she thinking? Where is she living? What is she saying to you? At the end of the timed writing, we simply went around the circle reading and listening to the new voices in our midst.

At that point in the day, I invited everyone to take all their writing and to begin to write a story that brought together the non-fictional grandmother with the woman they had just written about. I suggested that they start at any point and not think about traditional structures of stories. For example, it could be the voice of the last character, the object, or the narrator. They could start with some person or detail, then bring in something else and see what happened. I asked them to let ideas interact and not worry about endings or beginnings, just finding meaning between the pieces of writing.

After thirty minutes, the women regrouped and read their work completed to that point. They were clearly interested in how differently they were beginning to understand the women about whom they were writing and how much they had explored their own thoughts and emotions through this process.

I suggested we end the day with one final writing practice.

The work began by asking them to choose their four best sentences from the day. Then I shared a poem by Eavan Boland, "The Woman Turns Herself Into a Fish," that had the long, slim structure similar to the Richardson poem described in chapter 4. I asked the writers to work with their four sentences, using what they thought were the most powerful words and taking out whatever ones were not absolutely necessary. Finally, they arranged the sentences following the form of Boland's poem.

The day concluded with the women reading their poems and describing how much more deeply they felt connected to the women they had named at the beginning of the day and how the different processes of writing and interpretive practice had brought them new understanding about their relationship to their grandmother. They were astonished at how much writing they had accomplished with less effort than usual.

This remembered workshop highlights some of the possibilities arising from writing practices. The writing of different texts, some drawing from personal memory, others using fictional techniques, reveals the relationship among ideas and the connection of one's remembered experience to that which is imagined. Some of the images of the grandmothers, the sensory details of the texts, and the rhythms of the language reappeared in several of the pieces, showing a range of interpretations. The women had the opportunity to explore their relationship with their grandmothers from different dimensions. Interpretive practices help us to understand our experience anew and sometimes with more depth.

Another aspect of the writing practices was the awareness of voice and how our language is always "half someone else's." While we are less conscious of this process when we write autobiographically, when writing from someone else's perspective, we realize how the words are only partially our own. As the women wrote from the perspective of those in the pictures, they became more aware of how our writing voices are shaped and how they can be constructed and changed or reimagined.

Finally, the shift in forms also raised their awareness of how structures contribute to meaning. For instance, writing narratives first and then being asked to choose several lines to create a poem highlighted the kinds of interpretations possible within a form and across them, creating a kind of writing heuristic.

Writing practices are not limited to the examples I have given here. Even though there are an infinite number of possibilities as each group I work with develops new versions, I have identified three commonalities among those that I have used and those that I continue to develop.

First, every writing practice begins with some way for individuals to make a personal connection. This may be through flow writing, through oral storytelling, through the sharing of other art forms and so on. This personal connection forms the basis of the data with which we work.

Second, each writing practice involves a series of events with at least one shift to allow for interpretation. This shift may be one between media, genre or topic. For example, we may begin with flow writing, read a poem and then write a narrative connecting the two pieces. Or individuals might bring their favorite snapshot and write a narrative about the picture and then follow the pattern of an existing poem to turn their own work into poetry.

Third, writing practices involve liberating constraints. That is, the interpretive events must have enough structure to narrow the focus and bring people into the field about which they will write while still offering numerous possibilities for responding. As a writing teacher, the worst thing I could do was to say to my students "write whatever you want." Where does one begin?

Writing practices help put words on a page and overcome the terror of the blank page or screen; they help to interpret experience and reveal what was already known. Writing practices also can teach us how texts work and are a good starting place for creating critical awareness of language and textual structures.

Critical Awareness

I am choosing to call this approach "critical awareness" rather than critical literacy because the latter has several different meanings and each of those meanings carries a certain weight of history. Barton (1994) described the various interpretations of critical literacy as including critical thinking; subjecting terms to examination, analysis and deconstruction and creating a critical discourse; and as linking up with critical theory that questions social structures and the inequities in access and power.

In retaining the conception of "critical," however, I am recognizing the importance of such an approach with writing. Mary Talbot (1992) described looking at language critically as "a way of *denaturalizing* it—questioning and making strange conventions which usually seem perfectly natural to people who use them. It can help *empower* them in the sense of giving them greater conscious control over aspects of their lives, especially how language shapes them" (p. 174). This meaning is what I bring to critical awareness.

I have used a number of examples of how critical awareness developed within the writing groups. These and others can be organized into three types of activities. First are the deconstruction activities where the texts were opened up, questioned, read closely, or even dismantled into lists of words. Second, we used reinterpretation activities, a process such as retelling fairy tales from a feminist perspective. And finally, the sideshadowing process that I developed from Morson's work to raise writers' awareness of their texts.

Deconstruction

Deconstruction arises from the work of Jacques Derrida who critiqued the structuralist perspective. He questioned the hierarchal oppositions common in Western thought such as male/female and speech/writing among many others. Deconstruction shows that such oppositions are not natural and inevitable but are constructed and produced by discourses. In questioning the construction, deconstruction dismantles it and then reinscribes it; that is, gives it another structure and functioning (Culler, 1997). When brought to texts, deconstruction reveals that the language and structure are not inevitable, but are the result of particular choices and operations of power.

One of the initial activities that I like to do with writers is work with metaphor. As Lakoff and Johnson (1980) pointed out some time ago, our language is more metaphorical than we generally recognize, affecting our everyday understandings. For instance, we can consider the metaphor of time having monetary value through such statements as "You're wasting my time" or "How do you spend your time?" (Lakoff & Johnson, pp. 7–8). Sensory words used to describe writing are another good example of how commonplace metaphors really are. We ask someone to "say in writing what we discussed on the phone" (Barton, pp.17–18) or we "see what someone is saying."

By asking writers to pay attention (another metaphor there!) to the verbs and helping interpret the metaphoric assumptions of the language they are using, one can reveal a particular approach they are taking to their writing, including unconscious beliefs.

In her poem entitled "Essay On What I Think Most About," Anne Carson described the importance of metaphor as she reminded us that Aristotle had equated metaphors with the mind experiencing itself making a mistake. She explained how something will seem wrong and then suddenly make sense offering a moment of awareness. Her poem further suggested that metaphors can teach the mind to enjoy such mistakes as it learns from what is and is not the case. (2001, pp. 30–31).

Another process of deconstruction I have developed draws from Frigga Haug's work. When members of the group brought the stories of various parts of the body, Haug and her colleagues circulated and discussed them before the author rewrote. They searched for "absences in the text, for internal contradictions and for clichéd formulations covering knots of emotion or painful detail" (Carter, 1987, p. 13). This kind of focus on specific parts was the approach I described earlier with Alexis's text when we broke the girls' narratives into wishes, hope and dreams, and feelings. By taking the ideas out of the familiar syntactic structures, the power of the words themselves resonated.

A similar approach of "taking apart" a text occurred with my reading of the transcripts. While I did not physically dismantle the sentences, shifting the form into poetry opened up the text to be read differently. I could consider the context, what we had said, what we had not spoken or written, and what kinds of influences seemed to direct the group.

In using deconstruction to raise critical awareness, it is important to create some kind of activity to focus on specific parts, to dismantle what exists to understand its aspects differently. Such a process can be difficult to engage in because it sometimes seems disrespectful, yet by understanding more clearly what one is writing and the structures that influence such work and affect choices in language, one can be clearer about the texts she is creating. Greater awareness of the power structures at work means that one can make better informed choices in her writing.

Reinterpretations

Reinterpreting is often related to deconstruction since once we understand the workings of the text through such a process, we can "reinscribe" the text. There are other ways of reinterpreting, however. Bringing a different lens to read a text is one example, such as Irigaray's psychoanalytic reading of Plato's cave story.

In writing practices, a common activity that I ask individuals to do is write from another specified perspective, such as the women in the pictures. This process has a similar effect to thinking about something from a different theoretical perspective. Images and ideas that one may be blind to in one perspective seem obvious from another.

Another form of reinterpreting occurs when images, forms, and rhythms are used in a new context. Susan Friedman's "Craving Stories" outlined some of the possibilities for women doing this kind of writing. The images of the cave, too, that appeared in some of the girls' writing is another example of this process.

A reinterpretation activity also can invite writers to describe their experiences from another tone or rhythm of voice. Asking the young women to write the forbidden opened up an interesting torrent of images and stories. I have attended a workshop where the poet asked us to write the dangerous, to write what we had never dared before. I took up her invitation and was deeply shaken by the words that poured from my pen. I did not know I was even thinking such things.

Reinterpreting a text, telling a story differently, shining another light on an image, or finding another tone or rhythm of voice are important ways of calling into question what seems solid and unchanging and reveals the spaces where the new can emerge.

Sideshadowing

In some of my recent work with writing groups, I have arranged to meet with each writer individually to have an extended discussion about her text. While I originally developed this process as a way of gathering writing data, I soon realized that it offered an opportunity for the writer to develop more insight about her text and for me to document this process of becoming aware.

I was interested in the decisions they made while writing. I also asked them about other decisions they might have made. Why did they use this character and not another? Why did they feel the need to describe this landscape in such detail? How did shifting forms of writing help them realize some of those possibilities? I wondered.

I earlier mentioned Morson's conception of sideshadowing, but I would like to return to his ideas to elaborate further my use of this technique. Morson explained that narratives have worked very well to create a single line out of a multiplicity of alternatives. But in doing so, we have tended to give an anachronistic sense to the past, shutting down the more complex and plural nature of experience. He suggested approaching texts with a sense of 'sideshadowing' to rediscover the multiplicity of interpretation.

> Instead of casting a foreshadow from the future, it casts a shadow 'from the side,' that is, from the other possibilities. Along with an event, we see its alternatives; with each present, another possible present. Sideshadows conjure the ghostly presence of might-have-beens or might-bes. While we see what did happen, we also see the image of what else could have happened. In this way, the hypothetical shows through the actual and so achieves its own shadowy kind of existence in the text. (1994, p. 118)

To prepare for a sideshadowing interview I read the work that the writer had chosen to discuss with me and marked places where I wondered about words they had chosen, where I found myself thinking about what was not said, or where I saw interesting figurative devices. I noted choices of line break, places where rhythm shifted or faltered, and images that were particularly striking. I engaged in what Jane Gallop (2000) called "close reading." Gallop argued that an ethical way to read another's work is to put one's own assumptions and interpretations to one side as she closely pays attention to the rhythms, images, and syntax of the writer. She described the process as one of staying with the text and what exists on the page rather than leaping to conclusions. By rereading the writer's text and making notes in the margin, I could give closer attention to what was in front of me.

I presented an example of sideshadowing in chapter 4. In that instance, the young woman described an experience of breaking up with her boyfriend in a train station. Her most telling line—"Before she could move in for the kill"—seemed to point to a depth of emotion about this event, reflecting the anger that women are discouraged from expressing. Yet in dreams, slips of the tongue, or our writing, we catch sight of the unconscious, which is aware of far more than our conscious mind recognizes. In paying attention to the words, the connotative character of language is clearer.

Writers know that language can be ambiguous and this can make us hesitant, certain that we will be misunderstood about those important moments we write on the page. At the same time, the ambiguity of language lets us slip and slide, hiding behind our own intentions in creating a text. Spending time in careful attention, casting a light with another spills the sideshadow across the page and in that moment, we can break the singular line of the narrative into threads of possibility.

Sideshadowing admits, in addition to actualities and impossibilities, a *middle realm* of real possibilities that could have happened even if they did not .... By focusing on the middle realm of possibilities, by exploring its relation to actual events, and by attending to the fact that things could have been different, sideshadowing deepens our sense of the openness of time. It has profound implications for our understanding of history and of our own lives while affecting the ways in which we judge our present situation. It also encourages skepticism about our ability to know the future and the wisdom of projecting straight lines from current trends or values. (Morson, 1994, p. 6)

By exploring this middle realm in our writing, we experience the subjunctive space of writing, imagining new possibilities and considering new interpretations. The best structures for this awareness to develop were the writing groups where we could focus our attention on the writing, engage in conversation about the work, and help each other come to understand.

Heard Into Speech

bell hooks wrote: "Even though writing is a solitary act, when I sit with words that I trust will be read by someone, I know that I can never be truly alone. There is always someone who waits for the words, eager to embrace them and hold them close" (1999, p. 11). hooks described the sense of trust that she will be heard, that someone will want to listen.

For those beginning to write in a way that expresses their personal experience and feelings, this sense of trust may not be present. As Nelle Morton explained about her consciousness-raising groups for women, this trust developed as they were heard. What was important, according to her, was the creation of structures for this hearing to happen and for the trust to grow.

I have found it interesting to return to the recent history of some of the feminist work of the 1970s, a decade when there seemed to be an explosion of conversations among women and pressure for change in society. In reading Nelle Morton's work with small groups, I have found that the patterns she observed then are relevant to what occurred in my writing groups. She noted that "the core of what is taking place in the woman [*sic*] movement is revealed most vividly and poignantly in small intimate groups" (1985, p. 13). The possibilities for change occur within and among individuals in such a setting and though those events may seem small and insignificant, change can happen one moment at a time.

Morton described consciousness-raising groups as offering the opportunity for women to become conscious of their lives. For women, "it is the coming to awareness of herself, her identity as a human person with the rights, responsibilities, and potentials thereof in light of her unexamined, traditionally accepted position in present and historical situations" (p. 13). In my groups, through writing and conversation, women were able to see, to some degree, how the definitions of the female role create boundaries on acting and being.

In Morton's groups, she noticed defensiveness, hurt, anger and sadness as the women began to explore their situations. As we did through the writing, they questioned the use of words, especially those that seemed obviously male oriented and they challenged structures that seemed to favor men, such as the hierarchical and authoritative framework. They also examined the images that interpreted female experience. Morton noted how images are more powerful than concepts because they are less easily controlled. "Images refer to that entity which rises out of conscious and unconscious lives individually and in community that may shape styles of life long before conceptualization takes place" (p. 20). An examination of metaphors and symbols and other visual representations helps to begin calling such images into question.

As women struggle to describe their experience and to examine the practices and structures of society, they needed a space to talk about those insights and to be heard. In Morton's groups, she suggested that the women "came to know they were called into being because someone had heard and the hearing drew forth their speech" (p. 29).

An important aspect of this hearing is listening without judgment. In the women's writing groups, with the exception of the teachers, we did not critique or suggest revision of one another's work. It was enough to create the space for words to be written, for the writers to have their voices really heard and for their thoughts and emotions to form the fabric of conversation in those groups. Too often, perhaps, we are focused on "making it better," and creating a product that meets some standard. And all this before we have learned to write with confidence and to hear our voices.

Within a setting where we are heard, where our words are taken seriously, we grow into articulation. I think about the difference to Emily Carr's work once she had a community who listened to her, and in particular, her close association and ongoing conversations with Lawren Harris. She was able to express to him the desires she had toward her painting and to know he understood when he offered helpful responses.

Engaging in writing practices together, raising our critical awareness of texts, and feeling the confidence to speak out offered new possibilities for writing, new ways of understanding our subjectivity, and perhaps changed the color of our future.

Moving Beyond

For some time in my own work as a writer and in my work with others, I recognized writing's potential for examining our lives, for understanding the influences and pressures about us, and for seeing the many connections to memory, experience and other texts. I was not satisfied in thinking about this work as "women's writing" because I felt that, while such a designation was appealing, it was one more box in which to confine women's experience. While I found the conception of social construction and poststructural theories helpful in questioning the definitions of women's roles and the practices associated with texts, I wanted a way to think about how change may actually begin to occur.

Hearing Elizabeth Grosz's paper where she proposed her conception of writing, thinking and reading otherwise—for women and for men—suggested the hopefulness for which I had been searching. As I considered how writing otherwise might come about, I was drawn to Cooper's notion of ecology, but found that I needed to move further to Abram's understanding of how language and writing is deeply connected to the natural world. Coupled with complexity theory, understanding writing in this way seemed richer and more productive to me.

An ecology supports diversity suggesting that there is no unifying consciousness for writers nor are there a limited modes of expression. We have perhaps mistaken the patterns of socialization for the way things have to be. Suggesting that our understanding is always in flux makes things less clear and creates uncertainty, but it also offers the possibility of a different future.

While writing otherwise still feels tentative and much of the hope unrealized, I have developed a sense of what it means for me at this point. Writing otherwise is to be aware of the constraints, to see the boundaries as well as the gaps where one can wiggle through to make the opening larger, to create a new space with a different view, to remember the sensory qualities of language. It asks us to work together to reconceptualize the world we live in, to find new language to describe our experience and those of others and to search for new structures of writing in which to represent our lives. Writing otherwise offers new ways of being but such work will be long, slow and ongoing. I believe I have seen glimpses and have ideas about how this might be possible, but like all things emerging, we can see the pattern more clearly as it unfolds behind us.

Writing otherwise means not knowing how it will all turn out. We only have to set out toward the unpredictable future, just as Carmen did not know how her journal writing would help her find a new life, just as the girls did not know how some of their beliefs would be challenged and just as my friends never know how opportunities to write will continue. bell hooks said: "We write because language is the way we keep a hold on life" (p. 13). I imagine that we can write to lessen that hold a bit and bring a new world into being, one word at a time.

Notes

1. See also Luce-Kapler, R., Chin, J., O'Donnell, E.; Stoch, S. (March, 2001). The design of writing: Unfolding systems of meaning. *Changing English, 8* (1): 43–52.
2. To read this story in another context, see *Engaging Minds: Learning and Teaching in a Complex World,* B. Davis, D. Sumara & R. Luce-Kapler, 2000, p. 79.

references

Abram, D. (1996). *The spell of the sensuous: Perception and language in a more-than-human world.* New York: Pantheon Books.

Allen, P.G. (1983). *The women who owned the shadows.* San Francisco: Spinsters Ink.

Annas, P.J. (1987). Silences: Feminist language research and the teaching of writing. In C. Caywood & G. Overing (Eds.), *Teaching writing: Pedagogy, gender, and equity* (pp. 3–17). Albany: State University of New York.

Atwell, N. (1987). *In the middle: Writing, reading, and learning with adolescents.* Portsmouth, NH: Boynton/Cook Publishers.

Atwood, M. (1982). *Second words: Selected critical prose.* Toronto, ON: Anansi.

Bakhtin, M.M. (1981). *The dialogic imagination.* (M. Holquist, Ed.; C. Emerson & M. Holquist, Trans.). Austin: University of Texas Press.

Bamford, C. (2000). In the presence of death. In P. Zaleski (Ed.), *The best spiritual writing* (pp. 1–18). San Francisco: Harper.

Barton, D. (1994). *Literacy: An introduction to the ecology of written language.* Oxford, UK: Blackwell.

Bateson, G. (1982). Difference, double description and the interactive designation of self. In F.A. Hanson (Ed.), *Studies in symbolism and cultural communication* (pp. 3–8). Lawrence: University of Kansas.

Belenky, M.F., Clinchy, B.M., Goldberger, N.R., & Tarule, J. (1986). *Women's ways of knowing: The development of self, voice, and mind.* New York: Basic Books.

Blanchard, P. (1987). *The life of Emily Carr.* Vancouver, BC: Douglas & McIntyre.

Boland, E. (1990). The woman turns herself into a fish. In *Outside history: Selected poems, 1980–1990.* New York: W.W. Norton & Company.

Borgmann, A. (1992). *Crossing the postmodern divide.* IL: The University of Chicago Press.

Brandt, D. (1987). *Questions I asked my mother.* Winnipeg, MB: Turnstone Press.

Brandt, D. (1996). *Dancing naked: Narrative strategies for writing across centuries.* Stratford, ON: The Mercury Press.

Briggs, J., & Peat, D.F. (1999). *Seven life lessons of chaos: Timeless wisdom from the science of change.* New York: HarperCollins.

Bruffee, K. (1984). Collaborative learning and the "conversation of mankind." *College English, 46,* 635–652.

Bruner, J. (1986). *Actual minds, possible worlds.* Cambridge, MA: Harvard University Press.

Bruner, J. (1990). *Acts of meaning*. Cambridge, MA: Harvard University Press.

Cahnmann, M. (2003). The craft, practice, and possibility of poetry in educational research. *Educational Researcher, 32* (3), 29–36.

Calvino, I. (1989). The adventure of a poet. In *Difficult loves and Marcovalo* (W. Weaver, Trans.) (pp. 103–108). Toronto, ON: Lester & Orpen Dennys.

Capra, F. (1996). *The web of life: A new scientific understanding of living systems*. New York: Doubleday.

Carr, E. (1951). *Klee Wyck*. Toronto, ON: Clarke Irwin.

Carr, E. (1966). *Hundreds and Thousands: The journal of an artist*. Toronto, ON: Irwin.

Carson, A. (2001). *Men in the off hours*. Toronto, ON: Vintage.

Carter, E. (Trans.) (1987). Translator's forward. In F. Haug (Ed.), *Female sexualization*. London: Verso.

Chodorow, N. (1978). *The reproduction of mothering*. Berkeley: University of California Press.

Chopin, K. (1986). *The awakening and selected stories*. London: Penguin Books.

Cilliers, P. (1998). *Complexity and postmodernism: Understanding complex systems*. London: Routledge.

Cixous, H. (1991). *Coming to writing and other essays*. Cambridge, MA: Harvard University Press.

Cooper, M. (1986). The ecology of writing. *College English, 48,* 364–375.

Crozier, L. (1995). *Everything arrives at the light*. Toronto, ON: McClelland & Stewart.

Crusius, T.W. (1991). *A teacher's introduction to Philosophical Hermeneutics*. Urbana, IL: National Council of Teachers of English.

Culler, J. (1997). *Literary theory: A very short introduction*. GB: Oxford University Press.

Davies, B. (1992). Women's subjectivity and feminist stories. In C. Ellis & M. G. Flaherty (Eds.), *Investigating subjectivity: Research on lived experience* (pp. 53–76). London: Sage.

Davis, B. (2004). *Inventions of teaching: A genealogy*. Mahway, NJ: Lawrence Erlbaum Associates.

Davis, B., Sumara, D., & Luce-Kapler, R. (2000). *Engaging minds: Learning and teaching in a complex world*. Mahwah, NJ: Lawrence Erlbaum Associates.

DeSalvo, L. (1999). *Writing as a way of healing: How telling our stories transforms our lives*. San Francisco: Harper.

Doll, M.A. (2000). *Like letters in running water: A mythopoetics of curriculum.* Mahwah, NJ: Lawrence Erlbaum Associates.

DuPlessis, R.B. (1990). For the Etruscans. In *The pink guitar: Writing as feminist practice* (pp. 1–19). New York: Routledge.

Ede, L., & Lunsford, A. (1990). *Singular texts/plural authors: Perspectives on collaborative writing.* Carbondale: Southern Illinois University Press.

Elbow, P. (1973). *Writing without teachers.* GB: Oxford University Press.

Elliott, B., & Wallace, J. (1994). *Women artists and writers: Modernist (im)positionings.* London: Routledge.

Erdrich, L. (1994). *The bingo palace.* New York: HarperCollins.

Felski, R. (1989). *Beyond feminist aesthetics: Feminist literature and social change.* Cambridge, MA: Harvard University Press.

Finke, L.A. (1992). *Feminist theory, women's writing.* Ithaca, NY: Cornell University Press.

Flint, K. (1992). Introduction. In V. Woolf, *The waves.* London: Penguin Books.

Foucault, M. (1984). What is an author? In P. Rabinow (Ed.), *The Foucault reader.* New York: Pantheon Books.

Friedman, S. (1994). Craving stories: Narrative and lyric in contemporary theory and women's long poems. In L. Keller & C. Miller (Eds.), *Feminist measures: Soundings in poetry and theory* (pp. 15–42). Ann Arbor: University of Michigan Press.

Gadamer, H-G. (1979). *Truth and method.* (W. Glen-Doepel, Trans.). London: Sheed and Ward.

Gallop, J. (2000). The ethics of close reading: Close encounters. *Journal of Curriculum Theorizing, 17* (3), 7–17.

Gilbert, S., & Gubar, S. (1979). *Madwoman in the attic: The woman writer and the nineteenth-century literary imagination.* New Haven, CT: Yale University Press.

Gilligan, C. (1982). *In a different voice: Psychological theory and women's development.* Cambridge, MA: Harvard University Press.

Gilman, C.P. (1973) *The yellow wallpaper.* New York: The Feminist Press.

Goldberg, N. (1986). *Writing down the bones: Freeing the writer within.* Boston: Shambala Publications.

Goldberg, N. (1990). *Wild mind: Living the writer's life.* New York: Bantam Books.

Greene, M. (1995). *Releasing the imagination: Essays on education, the arts, and social change.* San Francisco: Jossey-Bass.

Grosz, E. (March, 2000). *Histories of the present and future: Feminism, power, bodies*. Paper presented at Queen's University, Kingston, Ontario.

Grumet, M. (1988). *Bitter milk: Women and teaching*. Amherst: University of Massachusetts Press.

Guillén, C. (1993). *The challenge of comparative literature* (C. Franzen, Trans.). Cambridge, MA: Harvard University Press.

Gunew, S. (1997). Authenticity and the writing cure. In S. Kemp & J. Squires, (Eds.), *Feminisms* (pp. 237–241). GB: Oxford University Press.

Haug, F. (Ed.). (1987). *Female sexualization* (E. Carter, Trans.). London: Verso.

Hayles, N.K. (1989). Chaos as orderly disorder: Shifting ground in contemporary literature and science. *New Literary History, 20*, 305–22.

Hirshfield, J. (1998). *Nine gates: Entering the mind of poetry*. New York: Harper.

Hohne, K., & Wussow, H. (Eds). (1994). Introduction. In *Dialogue of voices: Feminist literary theory and Bakhtin* (pp. vii–xxiii). Minneapolis: University of Minnesota Press.

Hollway, W. (1984). Gender difference and the production of subjectivity. In J. Henriques, W. Hollway, C. Urwin, C. Venn, & V. Walkerdine (Eds.), *Changing the subject: Psychology, social relations and subjectivity* (pp. 227–253). London: Metheun.

Hollway, W. (1989). *Subjectivity and method in psychology: Gender, meaning and science*. London: Sage.

hooks, b. (1999). Remembered rapture: The writer at work. New York: Henry Holt and Company.

Hughes, T. (1967). *Poetry in the making*. London: Faber & Faber.

Irigaray, L. (1991). *Marine lover of Friedrich Nietzsche* (G. Gill, Trans.). New York: Columbia University Press.

Iser, W. (1978). *The act of reading: A theory of aesthetic response*. Baltimore, MD: The Johns Hopkins University Press.

Kerby, A. (1991). *Narrative and the self*. Indianapolis: Indiana University Press.

Klepfisz, I. (1982). *Keeper of accounts*. Watertown, MA: Persephone Press.

Kohlberg, L. (1984). *The psychology of moral development*. New York: Harper & Row.

Kristeva, J. (1980). *Desire in language: A semiotic approach to art and literature* (L.S. Roudiez, Ed.; T. Gora, A. Jardine, & L.S. Roudiez, Trans.). New York: Columbia University Press.

Langer, S. (1953/1967). *Feeling and form: A theory of art developed from Philosophy in a New Key*. London: Routledge & Kegan Paul.

Lakoff, G., & Johnson, M. (1980). *Metaphors we live by*. IL: University of

Chicago Press.

Lee, D. (1998). *Body music.* Toronto, ON: Anansi.

LeGuin, U.K. (1989). *Dancing at the edge of the world: Thoughts on words, women, places.* New York: Harper & Row.

Lessing, D. (1972). *The golden notebook.* London: Flamingo.

Luce-Kapler, R. (1994). Never stepping in the same river twice: Teaching and writing in school. Unpublished master's thesis, University of Alberta, Edmonton.

Luce-Kapler, R. (1997a). As if women writing. Unpublished doctoral dissertation, University of Alberta, Edmonton.

Luce-Kapler, R. (1997b). Reverberating the action research text. In T. Carson & D. Sumara (Eds.), *Action research as a living practice.* (pp. 187–198). New York: Peter Lang.

Luce-Kapler, R. (2000). Magnolia poems (Kate Chopin). *Journal of Curriculum Theorizing, 16* (4), 99–102.

Luce-Kapler, R. (2002). The breath of interpreting moments. In E. Mirochnik & D. Sherman (Eds.), *Passion and pedagogy.* (pp. 285–300). New York: Peter Lang.

Luce-Kapler, R. (2003). *The gardens where she dreams.* Ottawa, ON: Borealis Press.

Luce-Kapler, R., Chin, J., O'Donnell, E., & Stoch, S. (2001). The design of writing: Unfolding systems of meaning. *Changing English, 8* (1), 43–52.

Macrorie, K. (1970). *Telling writing.* Rochelle Park, NJ: Hayden.

McHugh, H. (1993). *Broken English: Poetry and partiality.* Hanover: University of New England Press.

Moffett, J. (1968). *Teaching the universe of discourse.* Boston: Houghton Mifflin.

Moi, T. (1985). *Sexual textual politics: Feminist literary theory.* London: Routledge.

Morson, G. (1994). *Narrative and freedom: The shadows of time.* New Haven, CT: Yale University Press.

Morson, G., & Emerson, C. (1990). *Mikhail Bakhtin: Creation of a prosaics.* CA: Stanford University Press.

Morrison, T. (1984). Memory, creation, and writing. *Thought, 89,* 385–390.

Morrison, T. (Dec. 1993). A Bird in the Hand is Worth Two in the Bush. Nobel Prize for Literature Acceptance Speech. Retrieved November 11, 2002, from http://www.nobel.se/literature/laureates/1993/morrison-lecture.html

Morton, N. (1985). *The journey is home.* Boston: Beacon Press.

Murray, D.M. (1985). *A teacher teaches writing* (2nd ed.). Boston: Houghton

Mifflin.

Oakley, A. (1972). *Sex, gender and society.* San Francisco: Harper & Row.

Olsen, T. (1978). *Silences.* New York: Delacourt Press.

Olson, D.R. (1994) *The world on paper: The conceptual and cognitive implications of writing and reading.* NY: Cambridge University Press.

Peacock, M. (1999). *How to read a poem ... and start a poetry circle.* Toronto, ON: McClelland & Stewart.

Philip, M.N. (1994). Dis place The space between. In L. Keller & C. Miller (Eds.), *Feminist measures: Soundings in poetry and theory* (pp. 287–316). Ann Arbor: University of Michigan Press.

Pound, E. (1951). *ABC of reading.* London: Faber.

Prigogine, I., & Stengers, I. (1984). *Order out of chaos: Man's new dialogue with nature.* New York: Bantam Books.

Prins, Y., & Shreiber, M. (Eds.) (1997). *Dwelling in possibility: Women poets and critics on poetry.* Ithaca, NY: Cornell University Press.

Radway, J.A. (1983). Women read the romance: The interaction of text and context. *Feminist Studies, 9,* 53–78.

Rich, A. (1979). *On lies, secrets, and silence.* New York: W.W. Norton & Company.

Richardson, L. (1997). *Fields of play: Constructing an academic life.* New Brunswick, NJ: Rutgers University Press.

Richardson, L. (2000). Writing: A method of inquiry. In N.K. Denzin & Y.S. Lincoln (Eds.), *Handbook of qualitative research.* 2nd ed. (pp. 923–948). Thousand Oaks, CA: Sage.

Rogers, M.F. (1991). *Novels, novelists, and readers: Toward a phenomenological sociology of literature.* Albany: State University of New York Press.

Salvio, P. (1999). Teacher of 'weird abundance': Portraits of the pedagogical tactics of Anne Sexton. *Cultural Studies, 13,* 639–660.

Scott, G. (1989). *Spaces like stairs.* Toronto, ON: The Women's Press.

Sedgwick, E. (1992). Gender criticism. In S. Greenblatt & G. Gunn (Eds.), *Redrawing the boundaries: The Transformation of English and American literary studies* (pp. 271–302). New York: Modern Language Association of America.

Shadbolt, D. (1990). *Emily Carr.* Vancouver, BC: Douglas & McIntyre.

Shields, C. (1993). Arriving late: Starting over. In J. Metcalf & J.R. Struthers (Eds.), *How stories mean* (pp. 244–251). Don Mills, Canada: General Publishing.

Shields, C. (2000). *Dressing up for the carnival.* Toronto, ON: Random House.

Showalter, E. (1989). *Speaking of gender.* New York: Routledge.

Showalter, E. (1994). *Sister's choice: Tradition and change in American Women's writing.* GB: Oxford University Press.

Smith, D.G. (2002). The mission of the hermeneutic scholar. In M. Wolfe (Ed.), *The mission of the scholar: Essays in honor of Nelson Haggerson* (n.p.). New York: Peter Lang.

Spigelman, C. (1998). Habits of mind: Historical configurations of textual ownership in peer writing groups. *College Composition and Communication, 49,* 234–255.

Sumara, D. (2002). *Why reading literature in school still matters: Imagination, interpretation, insight.* Mahwah, NJ: Lawrence Erlbaum Associates.

Sumara, D., Davis, B., & Luce-Kapler, R. (2000). Representing insight: Mapping literary anthropology with fractal forms. In T. Shanahan & F. V. Rodriguez-Brown (Eds.), *National Reading Conference yearbook* (pp. 534–549). Chicago: National Reading Conference.

Talbot, M. (1992). The construction of gender in a teenage magazine. In N.L. Fairclough (Ed.), *Critical language awareness.* London: Longman.

Tippett, M. (1979). *Emily Carr: A biography.* Toronto, ON: Oxford University Press.

Toth, E. (1999). *Unveiling Kate Chopin.* Jackson: University Press of Mississippi.

Usher, R., & Edwards, R. (1994). *Postmodernism and education.* London: Routledge.

Walker, B. (1983). *The woman's encyclopedia of myths and secrets.* San Francisco: Harper & Row.

Walton, K.L. (1990). *Mimesis as make-believe: On the foundation of the representational arts.* Cambridge, MA: Harvard University Press.

Weedon, C. (1987). *Feminist practice and poststructuralist theory.* New York: Basil Blackwell.

Welch, N. (1993). One student's many voices: Reading, writing and responding with Bakhtin. *Journal of Advanced Composition, 13.* Retrieved September 6, 2002, from http://jac.gsu.edu/jac/13.2/Articles/12htm

Welch, N. (1998). Sideshadowing teacher response. *College English, 60,* 374–395.

Whitehead, A.N. (1925). *An enquiry concerning the principles of natural knowledge.* Cambridge, GB: University Press.

Whitford, M. (1991a). Irigaray's body symbolic. *Hypatia Special Issue: Feminism and the Body, 6*(3), 97–110.

Whitford, M. (1991b). *Luce Irigaray: Philosophy in the feminine.* London: Routledge.

Winterson, J. (1989). *Sexing the cherry.* London: Vintage.

Winterson, J. (1995). *Art objects.* Toronto, ON: Alfred A. Knopf.

Woolf, V. (1929). *Room of one's own.* London: The Hogarth Press.

Woolf, V. (1938). *Three guineas.* London: The Hogarth Press.

Woolf, V. (1931/1992). *The waves.* London: Penguin.

Yaeger, P. (1988). *Honey-Mad women: Emancipatory struggles in women's writing.* New York: Columbia University Press.

index